Junior Encyclopedia of Australian
Wildlife

Author: Kylie Currey
Principal photographer: Steve Parish

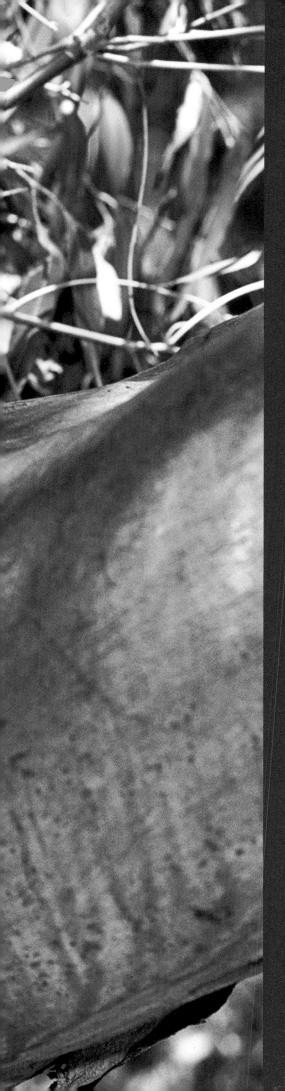

CONTENTS

Welcome
to the world of Australian wildlife

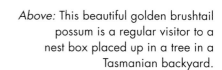

Australia is an island continent, separated from all other countries. It has over 35,000 kilometres of coastline, surrounded by oceans, and is home to many plants and animals that are found nowhere else on the planet.

More than two-thirds of Australia is very dry, or arid, desert. In fact, apart from icy-cold Antarctica where it hardly ever rains, Australia is the driest continent on Earth! But many Australian animals have developed fascinating ways to survive the harsh conditions of the arid inland. You don't need to travel to the centre of the continent to see Australia's amazing wildlife. Many animals can be found living in our parks and cities, in the bush, in forests and rainforests, and along the coast. If you take the time to look, listen, and even smell, you will discover that some of the creatures living in Australia may be as close as your own backyard!

One of the fabulous things about living in Australia is that, for many of us, seeing wildlife around the home or in the backyard is an everyday experience. Some animals, such as possums, are even cheeky enough to move in and make their home in the ceiling!

Steve Parish

Above: This beautiful golden brushtail possum is a regular visitor to a nest box placed up in a tree in a Tasmanian backyard.

Left: The world of Australian wildlife is filled with noise and colour, particularly when you come face-to-face with a flock of rainbow lorikeets.

The evolution
of Australian wildlife

Why is Australia's wildlife so different?

The pterosaur was a flying reptile.

Age of Dinosaurs

Dinosaurs were a group of reptiles that lived on land around 220 million years ago. They could not fly, but flying reptiles, like the pterosaur, lived at the same time.

Fossilised bones of *Minmi paravertebra*.

The Earth was a very different place 250 million years ago. All of the continents were joined together, forming a supercontinent called Pangaea. Around 180 million years ago, forces beneath the Earth's surface began to cause Pangaea to break into two pieces — Laurasia in the north and Gondwanaland in the south.

Over the next 130 million years Australia was part of a giant supercontinent called Gondwanaland — along with South America, India, Africa and Antarctica — and dinosaurs still roamed the planet! Over millions of years, Gondwanaland continued to break apart, the dinosaurs died out, and the Earth's climate went through many changes. Australia slowly drifted away from all other lands and became an island, and the animals and plants that survived experienced changes of their own. Today, much of Australia's wildlife is found nowhere else on Earth.

Preserving the past

Sometimes, the body of a dead animal is buried by mud or soil. If conditions are just right, over millions of years, the animal's bones may *fossilise*, or harden like a rock. Fossils can tell scientists how animals of the past looked and even what they ate!

Distant relatives

About 8 million years ago, *mega-fauna* (or "huge animals"), the relatives of modern-day Australian animals, evolved. Imagine 3-metre tall kangaroos hopping around, 500 kilogram birds hunting prey and 2 tonne, rhinoceros-sized marsupials grazing the plains!

Genyornis   *Procoptodon*

Parts of Australia may have looked like this during the Age of Dinosaurs.

Digging up the past

Palaeontologists are scientists who study fossils. They dig up and put together the pieces of an enormous puzzle to work out which animals roamed the planet many millions of years ago. It is exciting work discovering what the plants, animals and habitats of the time were like, and how prehistoric animals lived and behaved.

Palaeontologists dig carefully to uncover fossils.

Dromaeosaurs hunting the plant-eater *Muttaburrasaurus*.

Wildlife habitats

Where animals make their homes

Aside from icy Antarctica, Australia is the driest continent on the planet, but it is not all dry and desolate. It has many different habitats, from rugged coastlines and sandy beaches to snow-capped mountains, tropical rainforests, huge wetlands, winding rivers and wide open grasslands.

A habitat is a place where an animal makes its home. For an animal to be found naturally in a habitat, it must be able to stay alive there. It must be able to find enough food, water, oxygen and shelter to help it live, grow and produce young. Some animals can only survive in one type of habitat, while others can live in many different habitats across Australia.

Get out there!

Exploring the great outdoors is an excellent way for humans to experience and appreciate an animal's habitat. It is also the best way to get an inside look at animal life and how animals behave naturally in the wild.

Rocky cliffs

Whether they hop, fly, crawl or slither, lots of animals live, find food and hide from predators among rocky cliffs. Many have special feet or claws to help them grip smooth or rocky surfaces.

Deserts

Deserts and arid habitats are very hot and dry, but they are also alive with wildlife. The animals that live there mostly avoid the sun by living underground during the day or staying in the shade of small bushes.

Heathlands

Plants in the heathlands are usually short trees or shrubs. Heathlands grow close to the ocean or high in the mountains. They may be wet, dry, protected, or exposed to weather.

Coasts

Australia has 8222 islands and more than 35,000 kilometres of coastline. Many animals living along the coasts must survive salty conditions, sun, wind, and high and low tides.

Rainforests

Forests are probably home to more types of land animals than any other habitat. Animals live at every level, from below ground, in the leaf litter, and all the way up to the tree tops.

Rivers and streams

Some animals need a constant supply of water and live near or in large rivers and lakes. Many rivers, streams and wetlands dry up for part of the year. Animals living in these habitats must have ways to stop themselves drying out.

Woodlands

There are many different woodland habitats. Unlike in forests, the tree tops in woodland do not touch, which allows more sunlight to reach the forest floor. Possums and kangaroos live in woodlands.

The big picture

There are more insects on Earth than any other type of animal.

Where do they all fit in?

Most of the animals that we see moving around us every day make up only a very small part of the "big picture". Animals such as birds and mammals are far out-numbered by the little things in life, such as insects.

A world of discovery

Scientists believe there could be about 8 million invertebrates still to be discovered or named! New vertebrate animals are also being discovered all the time and there could be as many as 10,000 of them yet to be found.

Over a million different animals live on Earth and about 97 percent of them belong to the group known as *invertebrates*, which are animals that do not have a backbone, like worms and insects. The other 3 percent do have a backbone and are called *vertebrates*. Vertebrates are animals such as birds, fish, mammals, frogs, reptiles and humans.

If you grouped all of the species of animals into groups of 100, only three in each group would have a backbone!

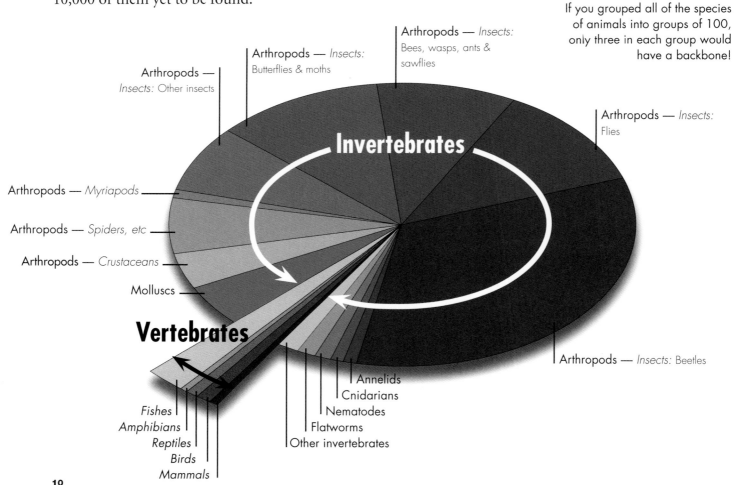

Arthropods — *Insects:* Other insects

Arthropods — *Insects:* Butterflies & moths

Arthropods — *Insects:* Bees, wasps, ants & sawflies

Arthropods — *Insects:* Flies

Arthropods — *Myriapods*

Arthropods — *Spiders, etc*

Arthropods — *Crustaceans*

Molluscs

Invertebrates

Vertebrates

Arthropods — *Insects:* Beetles

Annelids
Cnidarians
Nematodes
Flatworms
Other invertebrates

Fishes
Amphibians
Reptiles
Birds
Mammals

Grouping wildlife

From general to specific, kingdom to species

Scientists sort, or classify, animals into groups based on how similar they are. When doing this, they look at an animal's skeleton, its body covering, how it gives birth to young, how it behaves, and many of its other features.

Scientists use seven main levels to classify an animal. They start by placing all animals into one large, general group called a *kingdom*. Then they look at the similarities and differences between animals to sort them into groups called *phylum, class, order, family* and *genus* based on whether or not they think the animals are related to each other. Eventually, only one type, or *species*, of animal is left in each group. Each species is given a two-word Latin name. The first part of the name is the genus. This is a group of closely related animals with similar features. The second part is used only for that species of animal. All animals also have common names, which we use in this book, but these may be different around the world. An animal's scientific name is the same all over the world.

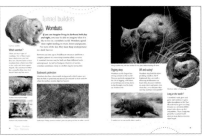

How the pages work

In this book, animals have been split into two groups: vertebrates and invertebrates. Similar animals have then been grouped firstly by phylum and then by class, as seen in the coloured text at the bottom of the page. The order, family, genus and species within a class may be included, but not the scientific names. All of the animals in this book are called by their common names, not their scientific names.

This is how scientists classify the eastern grey kangaroo. They begin with the very general group, the animal kingdom, and end with one group of animals, a species, with the two-word Latin name, *Macropus giganteus*.

Kingdom: Animalia — this includes all animals but not plants, bacteria or fungi.

Phylum: Chordata — animals with a nerve chord along the back. Includes humans, whales, snakes, kangaroos, wallabies, and wombats.

Class: Mammalia — warm-blooded vertebrate animals that produce milk. Includes humans, whales, wombats, kangaroos and wallabies, but not snakes.

Order: Diprotodontia — marsupial mammals that have one pair of lower incisor teeth. This includes kangaroos, wallabies and wombats, but not humans or whales.

Family: Macropodidae — animals from the order diprotodontia that have long hind feet. This includes only kangaroos and wallabies, not wombats.

Genus: *Macropus* — this genus name means "big-foot", and includes macropods with similar features, such as wallabies, wallaroos and other types of kangaroo.

Species: *giganteus* — this name means "gigantic". In the genus *Macropus*, only the eastern grey kangaroo is given the species name *giganteus*.

Vertebrates

Animals with backbones

Phylum: CHORDATA
Class: Mammalia — Mammals 14
Class: Aves — Birds 58
Class: Reptilia — Reptiles 94
Class: Amphibia — Amphibians 118
Class: Osteichthyes — Freshwater
 fishes 126

If you run your fingers down the centre of your back, you can feel the bones that join together to make up your spine, or backbone. Because you have a backbone, you belong to a large group of other animals with backbones — a group known as vertebrates!

Vertebrates make up only a very small number of all the different animals living on the planet. But, we are most familiar with vertebrate animals, firstly because we are vertebrates, but also because we can see them living all around us. We keep vertebrate animals such as dogs, cats and budgerigars as pets, and we take more notice of vertebrates because they are often cute and cuddly, big and scary, noisy or fast.

Top to bottom: Meeting a kangaroo; a crimson rosella; and a python.

Similar creatures

Humans are very different to kangaroos, parrots and snakes, but we are grouped into the same phylum — the phylum chordata — because, like all of these animals, a human has a backbone that contains a nerve cord running down it.

Mammals

Humans belong to a group of vertebrates known as mammals. One of the things that places mammals into one group is that they all must eat quite a lot of food on a regular basis. This is how mammals make sure they have enough energy to survive.

Tasmanian devil

Birds

There are more than 800 species of birds found throughout Australia. The bones of a bird's skeleton are hollow because most birds must have light bodies so they can fly. If a bird had a skeleton like a human, it would never get off the ground! Some large birds, like the emu and the cassowary, cannot fly at all.

Superb lyrebird

Reptiles

Some reptiles have hardly changed their body shape since the Age of Dinosaurs, over 200 million years ago! Unlike mammals, many reptiles can go without food for weeks, or even months. Their dry scaly skin allows them to live in some very hot, dry habitats.

Taipan

Amphibians

Amphibians are vertebrates that have an amazing two-part life cycle. The first part of an amphibian's life is spent in the water, where they are tadpoles that breathe through gills. As adults, amphibians live on dry land and breathe air through well-developed lungs, the lining of their mouth, their skin, or a combination of these.

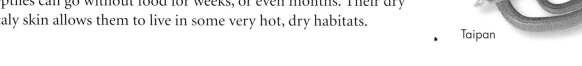

Orange-eyed tree-frog

Freshwater fishes

All fishes have gills and all but one, which is called a lungfish, can only breathe underwater. There are three different groups of fish. The first group is made up of jawless fishes, such as lampreys, which suck the blood of their prey. The second group is sharks and rays, which are fishes that have skeletons made of *cartilage*, a kind of tough, supportive tissue. The third group is for bony fishes, which have bony skeletons to support their bodies. Freshwater fish belong to the bony fishes group.

Coal grunter

Mammals
Animals with fur

Mammals are animals that have a body covered in fur, which is another name for hair. Furry coats help keep mammals warm. Besides fur, mammals have many other things in common — things that make them different to all other animal groups.

All mammals are warm-blooded. This means that their inside body temperature, which is the temperature of their blood, stays the same and doesn't become hotter or colder as the temperature of the outside air changes. Another word for this is *endothermic*, which means "heated from the inside".

Female mammals give birth to live young. They produce milk, which the babies drink from their mother's teat or nipple. Mammals can be divided into three groups depending on how they give birth. These groups are: monotremes, marsupials, and placental mammals.

Australia has many mammals that are unique because they are found nowhere else in the world!

Left: A little red flying-fox. *Below:* Common wombats.

Phylum: CHORDATA
Class: Mammalia
    Monotremes 16
    Marsupials 22
    Placental mammals 48

Mammals

Monotremes

For every rule there is always one exception, and monotremes are definitely the odd mammals out. They do not give birth to live young like other mammals, instead monotremes lay sticky, soft-shelled eggs!

Marsupials

Marsupials have two stages of development. First a baby marsupial develops inside its mother's tummy, and then inside her pouch or *marsupium*. A newborn baby marsupial is tiny. It has no fur, is blind, and has only stumps for back legs. It must pull its way through its mother's fur and climb into her pouch without any help. In the pouch it attaches to one of its mother's teats and continues to grow and develop as it drinks her milk, which has a lot of nutrients that the baby needs to help it grow.

Placental mammals

Baby placental mammals develop inside their mums' tummies along with a sac-like bag called a *placenta*. A special cord called the *umbilical cord* is attached from the placenta to the baby's bellybutton and helps the baby get vitamins and oxygen from its mother's blood. Placental mammals give birth to very well-developed young, complete with arms, legs, eyes, ears, nose and fur. Humans have bellybuttons because we are placental mammals!

Above, left to right: Short-beaked echidna; eastern grey kangaroo and joey; dingo. *Below:* Bottlenose dolphins.

Monotremes
The platypus and echidna

Like other mammals, monotremes are furry, warm-blooded and feed their babies milk. But unlike other mammals, platypuses and echidnas lay soft-shelled eggs and do not have teats!

After laying eggs, a mother monotreme keeps them warm, or *incubates* them, for about ten days until they hatch. Baby monotremes have an "egg-tooth", which is a sharp knob on their beaks that helps them break out of the eggshell. The egg-tooth falls off shortly after the monotreme hatches. A young monotreme has no fur at birth and as it grows it licks milk that oozes onto a patch of skin on its mother's belly.

Platypus

Platypuses are found only in Australia. A female lays up to three eggs at a time. After she has laid her eggs, the mother platypus lies on her back and incubates them between her tummy and her tail.

Echidna

About a month after mating, a female echidna lays one egg. Muscles around the two "milk patches" on her belly swell up to form a very simple pouch where the egg is protected until it hatches.

Left and above: Platypuses have a bill shaped like a duck's bill but softer.

Opposite: The echidna is sometimes called a spiny anteater.

An echidna's prickly spines help to protect it from predators.

Phylum: Chordata
Class: Mammalia

Secretive hunter

When diving, the platypus closes its eyes, ears and nostrils. It can stay hunting underwater for up to two minutes, but must come to the surface to eat its food and breathe air.

The platypus

Platypuses are shy and secretive. They prefer to live in unpolluted freshwater creeks in eastern Australia and usually venture out during the late afternoon, night and very early morning to feed.

A platypus uses its sensitive bill to feel for worms, yabbies, tadpoles and insects to eat. While it is underwater, a platypus stores its food in its cheeks until it comes to the surface to eat. Platypuses don't have teeth, instead they push their food to the back of the mouth, where it is ground and crunched up between the top and bottom jaws of the platypus's bill.

Resting and nesting

Platypuses dig burrows into creek banks about a metre above the water. There are two types of burrow — a *camping burrow*, where the platypus sleeps during the day, and a *nesting burrow* where the female goes to lay her eggs and raise her young until they are around 3–4 months old.

Webbed feet

The platypus is a strong swimmer. It uses its fully-webbed front feet to pull it through the water. The two back feet have some webbing, and with the help of the paddle-shaped tail, are used for steering. Male platypuses have a sharp, venomous 1.5-centimetre long spur on the ankles of their hind legs.

Sift and snap

As it swims, a platypus snaps its bill to grab passing prey, or uses it as a sieve to filter the bottom of the creek bed in search of small animals.

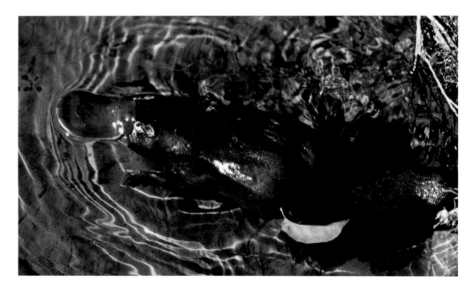

A platypus can grow to around 60 centimetres in length and weigh as much as 3 kilograms.

A platypus has two nostrils on its bill.

Phylum: Chordata
Class: Mammalia

This platypus is leaving its burrow to hunt in the water.

Oily fur

Platypus fur is very thick, soft and slightly oily. The oil helps keep the water out and the thick fur makes sure the platypus stays dry and warm, even when the water is very cold!

Platypus eggs are about 1.5 centimetres long, smaller than a twenty cent piece.

A platypus breathes through two nostrils on its bill.

A sixth, "electric" sense

A platypus hunts underwater with its eyes closed, so how does it find its prey? Its soft, rubbery bill is covered with very sensitive skin that is able to detect even the tiniest flicker of energy from electrical fields produced by the muscles of small creatures as they move under the water. This "electro-sensitivity" works like a sixth sense and lets the platypus know when to snap its bill.

The tail's tale

A platypus uses its tail as its lunch box! It stores fat in its tail that can be used to provide energy, or food, when underwater animals are hard to find. The platypus's tail becomes much thinner as it uses up its stored "food". Females can also use their tails to carry leaves, which they use to make a soft bed in the nesting chamber.

Spiky wanderer

The echidna is the only native mammal that can be found right across Australia.

An echidna can *camouflage* well in grass.

Echidnas are good escape artists.

Echidna protection

If threatened by a predator, an echidna rolls up into a prickly ball, or uses its claws to dig itself into the ground, disappearing so that only its spines can be seen!

The echidna

The short-beaked echidna is a ground-living mammal that is easily recognised by the pointy spines that cover its body. These sharp prickles provide excellent protection, and because their spiky armour is so good, echidnas have very few predators. In the wild they may live for up to 45 years!

Echidnas can be found wherever there is a good supply of their favourite foods — ants and termites. The best time to spot these secretive creatures is at dawn or dusk when they come out to search for food.

Echidnas live, and search for food, alone.

Prickly puggle

A baby echidna is called a *puggle*. After it hatches, it is carried in its mother's simple pouch. When the puggle begins to grow spines that tickle its mother's tummy just a bit too much, she digs a burrow and leaves it there while she goes out to search for food. Every few days, she returns to the burrow to give her puggle a drink of milk.

Phylum: Chordata
Class: Mammalia

A nose for all occasions

An echidna smells, breathes and eats through its nose, which is also called a snout. Insects collected by the animal's sticky tongue are taken into its tiny, toothless mouth, pushed to the back and ground up between the top and bottom jaws, ready to be swallowed. The echidna's nose also helps it in another way — when an echidna swims, it uses its back feet as paddles and its nose as a snorkel!

An echidna has a very long tongue.

Flick and stick

An echidna's tongue is about 18 centimetres long and covered in sticky saliva! It flickers in out of an ant or termite mound up to 100 times a minute, picking up insects and taking them back into the mouth for munching.

Above: Echidnas are good swimmers.
Right: An echidna drinking.
Below: Strong claws allow the echidna to dig burrows or escape underground, as well as to scratch open termite mounds and ant nests.

Marsupials
From tummy to pouch

Baby marsupials stay inside their mothers' tummies for only a very short amount of time. When they are born, baby marsupials, or joeys as they are called, are not fully formed and must finish their growth and development inside their mother's pouch, or *marsupium*.

The pouch protects the young joey and keeps it warm as it drinks milk from one of its mother's teats. A joey stays inside its mother's pouch until it is completely covered in fur. Only then will it begin to poke its head out and nibble solid food. Not all marsupials have a pouch. The numbat is one marsupial that doesn't carry and protect its young in a pouch.

Marsupial mole

The marsupial mole is totally blind — it doesn't even have eyes, simply because it does not need them! It spends most of its life underground, tunnelling through dry, sandy soil. Marsupial moles are carnivores that feed on insects such as beetles and ants. The female's pouch faces backwards so that sand shifted by her shovel-like claws does not fill the pouch and hurt the joey.

Above: The marsupial mole has no eyes.
Left: An allied rock-wallaby with her well-developed joey.

Phylum: Chordata
Class: Mammalia

Dasyuromorphia — the meat-eaters

Some marsupials are *carnivorous*, because they hunt and eat meat. They belong to the order Dasyuromorphia, which means "hairy tail shape". This group is split into two living families: the dasyurids (such as quolls, Tasmanian devils and smaller dasyurids), and the Myrmecobiidae family, whose only member is the numbat. The Tasmanian devil is the world's largest living marsupial carnivore.

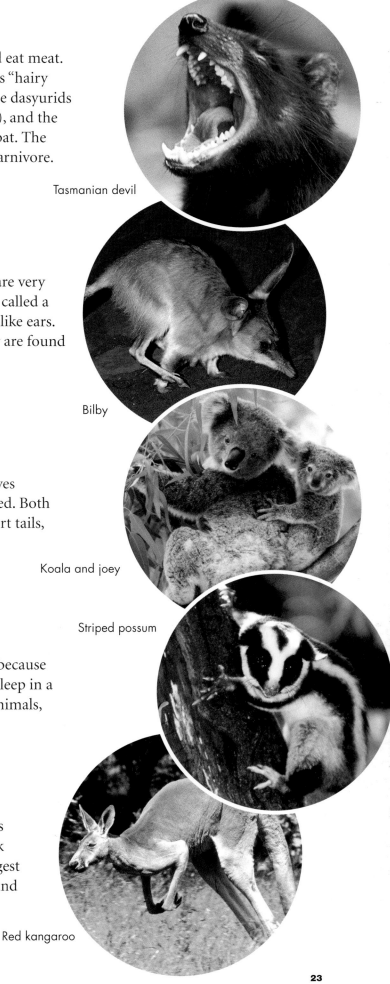

Tasmanian devil

Bandicoots and bilbies

Bandicoots and bilbies are long-footed marsupials that are very similar in looks and behaviour. In fact, the bilby is often called a rabbit-eared bandicoot because of its extra-long, rabbit-like ears. Bilbies once lived across most of Australia, but now they are found only in the dry sandy centre.

Bilby

Koalas and wombats

Although one spends its life in the trees and the other lives underground in a burrow, koalas and wombats are related. Both have pouches that open towards the back, both have short tails, and both are *herbivores* that eat only plants.

Koala and joey

Possums and gliders

Night time is the best time to spot possums and gliders because these tree-climbing marsupials spend most of the day asleep in a hollow. Most possums and gliders eat both plants and animals, so they are *omnivores*.

Striped possum

Kangaroos and their relatives

These marsupials are known as *macropods*, which means "big feet". They move by hopping on their powerful back legs and live in large family groups called mobs. The largest macropod in the world is the red kangaroo, which is found only in Australia.

Red kangaroo

Dunnarts are small, mouse-like dasyurids.

Fierce hunters
Small dasyurids

Australia's smallest mammals may look cute, but they are surprisingly ferocious hunters with sharp, needle-like teeth.

These meat-eating marsupials, known as dasyurids, sleep during the heat of the day and hunt under the cover of darkness when it is cool.

Many dasyurids don't have a "full-time" pouch like a kangaroo, but they do have a "part-time" pouch. When the female is ready to give birth, small folds of skin on her belly swell up and surround her teats. This protects her young as they drink her milk.

Bulging eyes

Dasyurids have big eyes to help them see in the dark as they hunt for spiders, insects and other small animals. Once they catch their prey, they use their front paws, like hands, to hold it while they chew.

A common planigale shows its teeth.

Munch and crunch

Small dasyurids have pointy noses, long whiskers and sharp, pointed teeth. A common planigale can grow up to 10 centimetres long and can devour insects as large as itself!

Mulgaras munch on insects and spiders.

Saving food for later

When there is plenty of food around, some dasyurids save food for later. They eat and eat and eat, and store all of their excess body fat in their tails. The fat is then used as a source of energy when food is hard to find.

Phylum: Chordata
Class: Mammalia

Little babies

The newborn babies of these marsupials can be miniscule! A mother usually gives birth to more babies than she has teats, so only the first to reach the pouch and attach themselves to a nipple survive.

Folds of swollen skin create a tiny "pouch" to protect baby phascogales as they drink their mother's milk.

Fantastic tree-climbers

Brush-tailed phascogales have long, fluffy tails that look like bottlebrushes. They are excellent climbers and spend the night darting along branches in search of insects, centipedes and spiders. Using their sharp front teeth, they peel back tree bark to surprise hiding prey.

Top: A brush-tailed phascogale making a meal of a grasshopper. *Above right:* The brush-tailed phascogale has a very bushy tail.

Life is short

Male phascogales have a very short life span — they only live for one year! During their first breeding season, they spend so much energy looking for females and mating that they die from exhaustion!

Spotted hunters

Northern quoll

Small and ferocious

The smallest of the quolls, the northern quoll, is also the most aggressive. It lives and hunts in woodlands and rocky places for small mammals, reptiles, insects and frogs. Unfortunately, this quoll is often poisoned by cane toads, which it mistakes for the harmless frogs it likes to eat.

Cane toad

Threats to quolls

Quolls once lived across most of Australia but their numbers have now decreased a lot. Larger, introduced predators, like cats, foxes and dingoes, eat them, and clearing bushland destroys their homes. The poisonous cane toad also leads to the death of any quoll that eats it thinking it is a tasty frog.

Quolls

Quolls are fierce, nocturnal carnivores with big, bright eyes and excellent eyesight. They hunt animals, but also eat fruit and scavenge *carrion*, which means they eat the bodies of dead animals. During the day, these night-time hunters sleep in a den inside a cave, hollow log or tree branch, or even in an old termite mound.

There are four types of quoll in Australia and, behind the Tasmanian devil, the spotted-tailed quoll is the second-largest carnivorous marsupial in the world. The spots on a quoll's furry coat look like "moon spots" and help it blend in with patches of moonlight on the forest floor.

The western quoll, or chuditch, has padded ridges on its back feet for extra grip while climbing.

Clever climbers

All quolls except for the eastern quoll have a "thumb" on each back foot for extra grip. This helps them to climb along smooth tree branches and over slippery rocks.

Phylum: Chordata
Class: Mammalia

Family life

A female quoll usually raises a litter of up to six pups. While they are small, she carries them around in her "part-time" pouch. When they become too large for the pouch, she carries them on her back or leaves them in a grass-lined den while she goes hunting.

Left: An eastern quoll with her pups.

Beach tracks

Tasmania is the only place in Australia where eastern quolls can still be found in the wild, and it is always exciting to find their tracks! A quoll sometimes leaves its paw prints in the sand as it searches for food along the high-tide mark.

The eastern quoll sometimes leaves tracks on the beach.

Spotted-tailed quoll

Size and power

The "king kong" of the quolls, the spotted-tailed quoll, has powerful arms and legs, strong claws and many sharp teeth. It can weigh up to 7 kilograms and catch prey the size of a wallaby! It is the only quoll that has spots on its tail.

Feral-free zone

The eastern quoll is thought to be extinct on the mainland, but some "released" quolls can be found living in natural surroundings protected by a feral-proof fence. If quolls are put back into the habitat they lived in, and are fenced in so that foxes are kept out, they live and breed naturally.

Scary scavengers

Tasmanian devils

With its bright red ears and spine-chilling screeches, it is no wonder the world's largest marsupial carnivore was given the name "devil". These nocturnal meat-eaters live only in the State of Tasmania, which is why they are called Tasmanian devils.

Jaws of steel

The large, wide head and jaws of a Tasmanian devil are very powerful. Its strong teeth and jaws crunch up every-thing, even bones! In just half an hour, a devil can chomp through meat that weighs almost half of its own body weight!

Devils squabble noisily around food, which may make them look and sound scary, but they are really quite shy! They can hunt prey the size of a wombat, but often prefer to scavenge. By eating dead carcasses, devils help keep the bush clean.

Young Tasmanian devils snuggle up together in their den.

Young devils play-fighting.

Bossy little beasts

While growing up, young devils play-fight and practise showing who's boss. When mother devil returns to the den from her night of hunting, the bossiest little devil normally gets the most food!

Devils in the den

A mother devil may carry up to four young, or joeys, in her back-wards-facing pouch. Once the joeys grow fur, she leaves them in the den while she heads out in search of food to bring back. At around eight months of age, young devils leave the den to live and hunt on their own. A devil may travel up to 16 kilometres each night in search of food.

Phylum: Chordata
Class: Mammalia

A mother devil brings food back to the den to feed her young.

A State icon

There are over 100,000 devils living throughout Tasmania, from high in the mountains to down along the coast. Devils are also very comfortable living around humans, on farms and even in the suburbs. In fact, they will live wherever they can scavenge food!

Above left:
Hearing and smell are the devil's most important senses when searching for food.

Devilish displays

When a group of devils gather around a carcass, it can be a very noisy scene indeed. There is a lot of snapping, snarling, coughing and growling — but it's really all just a big show! This is how devils work out a "pecking order" because the loudest, scariest devil gets first bite of the night's catch.

Left: The dark colour of a devil's fur helps it camouflage when it hunts at night.

Daytime diggers

Camouflage

The numbat's colours, stripy fur and fluffy tail help it to blend in with its grassy habitat.

Numbats

Unlike many marsupials, the colourful, fluffy-tailed Numbat is diurnal, or active during the daytime. It has a very special diet — it only eats termites!

Numbats were once the world's most endangered mammal and were in danger of becoming *extinct*, which means that they would never exist in the wild again. Fortunately, with the help of people protecting their homes and keeping feral foxes away, numbat numbers are slowly growing.

The numbat is a colourful marsupial.

Above, left to right: A busy numbat can eat up to 20,000 termites a day!

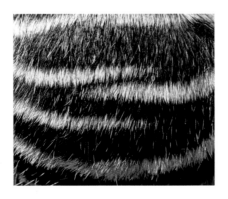

Nose to the ground

When hunting, a numbat is "head down, tail up". It finds a termite nest by using its excellent sense of smell. Then, it stops to dig small holes or overturn branches to uncover the colony hiding just below the ground. Numbats use their long, sticky tongue to flick and lick up termites.

Left: You can easily identify a numbat by the 4–11 white stripes that run across its back.

Phylum: Chordata
Class: Mammalia

These four baby numbats will stay attached to their mother's teats for around five months.

No pouch

Unlike other marsupials, a numbat doesn't have a pouch. It doesn't even develop a "part-time" pouch. Baby numbats attach themselves to their mother's teats and are carried or dragged around as they grow. When they become too big, they are carried on their mother's back or left in a nursery burrow on a soft nest of leaves, bark, grass and flowers.

Above: While their mother is hunting, these baby numbats play outside their burrow.
Below: Numbats are good climbers that live in hollow tree trunks.

Hollow home

Like humans, numbats sleep during the night time. They make their home in a hollow, or empty space in a tree trunk or fallen branch. To protect themselves from predators such as a sneaky fox or a large carpet python, numbats search for thin hollows that the predators might not be able to fit into.

A numbat's bottom is covered by very thick, tough skin. Because this skin is too thick to bite through or grab hold of, the numbat can use its bottom to "plug" the entrance to the hollow and keep out predators.

Super senses

A northern brown bandicoot feeding on a large grasshopper.

Bandicoots and bilbies

Both bandicoots and the bilby, which is a type of bandicoot, are marsupials that search for food at night. They rely on their excellent senses of smell and hearing to help them find food.

Bandicoots and bilbies use their strong front paws for digging. They have powerful back legs and long feet like a kangaroo, but rather than hop, they run and scurry along the ground on all fours.

On the hunt

Bandicoots and bilbies are omnivores, which means they eat both animals and plants. As cute as they may look, these marsupials have a set of sharp, needle-like teeth. They hunt for insects, spiders, centipedes, fruit and seeds. Bilbies also eat lizards and other small mammals.

The southern brown bandicoot eats insects, fungi and plant roots.

Scratch and sniff

A bandicoot uses its long nose to help it get its dinner. First, it digs a cone-shaped hole in the ground. Then, it pokes its nose into the hole in search of earthworms and insects. That's why its nose is often covered in dirt and sand!

Campsite foraging

If you're out camping in the bush, you may be lucky enough to see a bandicoot snooping around the campsite looking for leftovers!

A long-nosed bandicoot.

Phylum: Chordata
Class: Mammalia

Bilbies dig for grubs and plant roots.

Topsy-turvy pouch

Both bandicoots and the bilby have an "upside-down" pouch, which opens towards their tail-end rather than at the front. This helps stop dirt and sticks entering the pouch, and protects the young while their mother digs her burrow or scratches for food. Using their powerful front legs and claws, bilbies dig an underground burrow up to 3 metres long. This is where they sleep during the day before coming out after dark to feed.

Keeping their cool

Life in the desert is very hot, but a bilby's long, thin ears actually help it keep its cool! Its ears are covered in a very thin layer of skin, so blood flows just below the surface and passes very close to the outside air. As blood travels through the long ears it begins to cool down, and by the time it moves back into the bilby's body it is much cooler.

Koalas

Long claws help koalas grip branches as they climb.

Equipped to grip

Koalas are great climbers. They have special fingers and toes with sharp claws to help them cling tightly onto trees. Each of a koala's hands has two thumbs for extra grip, while the big toe on the inside of each foot helps the koala keep its balance as it climbs.

Koalas sometimes jump between branches.

Leap for leaves

Koalas are more acrobatic and agile than they look. They often leap from branch to branch in the tree tops. Travelling through the trees in this way means they don't have to go down to the ground, where predators may lurk.

Koalas have rounded bodies, soft fur and fluffy ears, and could easily be mistaken for the "teddy bears" of the bush. But, don't be fooled! A koala is not a bear — it is a marsupial and has a pouch.

You won't find a koala in the rainforest or in the desert. They only live in eucalypt forests where they dine on their favourite food, gum leaves. During the day they sleep perched in the low fork of a tree, heading up to the tree tops at night to feed.

A koala rests in the fork of a tree.

What's that sound?

Is it a grunt? Is it a snore? Is it a burp? It could be any or all of those sounds, because they are all made by the koala, especially during breeding season! Koalas also call to each other and their call is known as a *bellow*.

Koalas make some very unexpected sounds.

Phylum: Chordata
Class: Mammalia

Any old leaf simply won't do! Koalas are fussy when choosing gum leaves to eat.

Sleepy fuss-pots

There are more than 700 different types of gum trees, or eucalypts, in Australia, but koalas only like the taste of the leaves on a few of these types of trees. Gum leaves are very low in nutrients and don't supply koalas with much energy at all. Because of the low nutritional value of gum leaves, koalas must spend up to 20 hours a day resting and sleeping. In fact, an adult koala needs to eat about 1 kilogram of gum leaves each day to have enough energy to move around for a few hours at night!

Southern koalas have darker fur to soak up warmth from the sun.

North and south

Koalas in cooler southern areas are larger, darker and fluffier to help protect them from the cold. Northern koalas live where it is warmer and have lighter-coloured grey fur.

Male koalas have scent glands.

What's that mark?

Male koalas have a brown stain in the centre of their chests, caused by a smelly oil that oozes from a patch of skin just below. A male rubs his chest along the branches of his "home" trees and uses the oil's smell to let other males know the boundaries of his area.

Above: This orphaned pouch joey is now being hand-reared.

Above and right: Mother koalas teach joeys which leaves to choose.

Water in the leaves

Except for in times of drought, koalas don't need to drink water because they get all the moisture they need from the fresh, juicy gum leaves they eat!

Baby joeys

Female koalas usually give birth to one hairless joey each year. This tiny, pink, jelly-bean-sized baby climbs into the mother's backwards-facing pouch where it stays attached to the teat, drinking milk. Only when it is covered in fur does the joey begin to poke its head out to nibble leaves. The joey doesn't fall out when the mother climbs because, using a muscle at the opening of the pouch, mother koalas can close their pouch like a draw-string bag! This way the joey can't get out, and sticks can't poke in while the mother is climbing.

Left: This joey is about one month old and is still hairless.

When it grows too big for the pouch, a baby koala climbs onto its mother's back.

Mother koalas cuddle their babies to keep them warm.

Motherly care

After about seven months, a baby koala has just about grown too big for the pouch and rides "piggy-back" on its mother instead. At this stage, the mother koala begins to teach her baby survival skills. The young koala stays under the protection of its mother until it is about one year old.

The wedge-tailed eagle preys on baby koalas.

Danger on foot

When gum trees are close together, koalas can jump from tree to tree through the branches and there is no need for them to come down to the ground. But when a koala needs to move along the ground, life becomes a lot more dangerous! Dingoes, large goannas, predatory birds and snakes all hunt baby koalas, especially those not protected by their mothers. Even when they are with mum, babies are not always safe. Many koalas have to cross roads and cars are a big danger. Koalas are also open to attack by dogs and large cats in suburban areas.

Tunnel builders

Wombats

Common wombat

If you can imagine living in darkness both day and night, you may be able to imagine what it is like to live in a wombat's world. Wombats spend their nights feeding on roots, leaves and grasses. For most of the day, they sleep deep underground in a dark burrow.

Burrows can have up to 20 different entrances and form a complex pattern of connecting tunnels, called a *warren*. A wombat's burrow may be built on three different levels underground. As well as living in a burrow or warren, wombats sometimes sleep in a hollow log for protection.

Which wombat?

There are three types of wombats. Two of these types have a hairy nose, and one does not. The two hairy-nosed wombats have a hairy nose that is also wider and more square-shaped. The common wombat has a smooth, shiny nose that doesn't have any hair on it.

Backwards protection

Wombats also have a backwards-facing pouch, which makes sure that the baby is protected and doesn't get covered in sticks and dirt when the mother wombat digs her burrow.

Southern hairy-nosed wombat

Northern hairy-nosed wombat

Peek-a-boo! A baby common wombat's paws are poking out from its mother's pouch.

Phylum: Chordata
Class: Mammalia

Young wombats stay with their mothers for two years before heading off alone.

Digging deep

Wombats are the largest burrowing animals in the world! They are perfectly equipped for the job of digging, with short, powerful legs and strong claws to dig through even the hardest, stoniest soils.

Off and racing!

Wombats may look like slow, plodding waddlers, but if frightened they can reach a blistering 40 kilometres an hour! Also, because wombats are quite short and squat, even when they are at full pace they can stop and turn very quickly!

A wombat can run very quickly when it needs to.

Wombats shelter in hollow logs.

Long in the tooth?

A wombat's teeth grow and grow, and continue to grow right throughout its life! But the teeth never grow too long because as a wombat nibbles grass it also chews up dirt and pebbles. These rough bits grind the wombat's teeth down to keep them at just the right length.

Treetop acrobats

The Leadbeater's possum has a very small gliding skin.

Possums and gliders

Rediscovered

For many years the Leadbeater's possum was thought to be extinct. But in 1961, they were rediscovered in the mountains of Victoria. Numbers are still low and the Leadbeater's possum is still endangered. The Leadbeater's possum has small folds of gliding skin, but does not glide.

Possums are "nocturnal", so they are only active at night. Their days are spent asleep in a hollow tree branch or nest of leaves. Like other tree-living mammals, they have sharp claws that help them cling to smooth bark as they climb.

Some possums have very strong, long tails, called *prehensile* tails because they can act like an extra arm and hold onto a branch. To add extra grip, prehensile tails have no fur on the underside. Gliders are a type of possum that seem to parachute through the air.

A feathertail glider.

Feathertail glider

At just 8 centimetres long, this is Australia's smallest gliding possum. It is also the smallest gliding mammal in the world! Tiny, stiff hairs poke out from the glider's tail, giving it a feathery look — and also its name.

Food from flowers

Some types of pygmy-possums munch on insects and sometimes lizards. Honey possums only eat nectar, and for this reason, are called *nectarivores*. With their brush-tipped tongues they soak up nectar, and they use a monkey-grip to hold small twigs. Eastern pygmy-possums also like to lick sugary nectar.

Eastern pygmy-possums

Itsy-bitsy babies

Adult pygmy-possums are the smallest of Australia's possums, at just over 5 centimetres long. Baby pygmy-possums develop in a pouch that opens at the top, like that of a kangaroo. But baby honey possums are even tinier! Honey possums have the smallest babies of all mammals.

Honey possums eat sweet nectar from flowers.

Phylum: Chordata
Class: Mammalia

40

Gliders in the night

When you see these possums moving through the air, it is obvious why they are called gliders. A thin flap of skin, called a *patagium*, stretches from the last finger on each hand down to the ankle. When a glider jumps between trees, it spreads its arms and legs and the flaps of skin stretch out and work like a parachute. A glider's long fluffy tail is not prehensile, so it can't be used to grip branches; instead, it acts like the rudder of a boat and helps steer the glider through the air.

A female squirrel glider's pouch is visible when she glides.

"Big" gliders

Gliding through the air, rather than running along the ground, helps gliders save energy. The yellow-bellied glider can glide up to 120 metres at a time as it jumps from gum tree to gum tree. The greater glider is the largest of the world's gliding mammals but it can only cover distances of up to 100 metres wide when gliding through the forest. Greater gliders can turn very sharply while in mid-air.

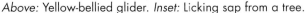

Above: Yellow-bellied glider. *Inset:* Licking sap from a tree.

The greater glider feeds on gum leaves.

A common brushtail possum and its baby find a tasty treat on a verandah.

Backyard visitors

There are many types of ringtail possum, but one, the common ringtail, can often be found living in people's backyards, where they search for fruit and flowers. To help them get down from the tree tops, ringtails often gallop across the roof, and if the roof is made of tin their pattering paws sound like thunderous thumps!

Ring grip

Most ringtail possums use their curly prehensile tail as a fifth arm to help them climb along branches and collect sticks and shredded bark to make their nests. If they slip from a branch, they simply pull themselves back up using their strong tail like a rope.

Double digits

The fingers and toes of many animals are known as *digits*. The first two digits on the front paws of ringtail possums can spread away from the other three to work like the two thumbs of a koala. Having digits clutching both sides of the branch helps possums hold tightly onto smooth bark.

A Herbert River ringtail possum.

Common and mountain brushtail possums

Common and mountain brushtail possums usually look very similar, but mountain brushtails are heavier, with shorter ears. Both of these types of possums have tails that look like a bottlebrush, but their tails are actually very strong and prehensile, so brushtail possums can use their tails like an extra arm.

Mountain brushtail possums can hang by their strong tails.

Ringtail possums

These possums got their name because of their tail which, when not being used, curls up into a coiled, ring shape. They build a round nest, called a *drey* in a tree hollow or forked branch and line it with leaves carried using their tail.

The common ringtail possum lives across eastern Australia.

The cuscus

The spotted cuscus is a slow climber, but it is no sloth! It lives in rainforest habitat, but doesn't sleep in a hollow, instead it pulls small leafy branches across a larger branch to form a bed, where it spends the day well-hidden. To stay cool, a cuscus pants like a dog and licks its face and feet.

The common spotted cuscus has a curly tail, similar to a ringtail possum's tail.

43

"Spring-loaded" legs

The second-largest macropod, the eastern grey kangaroo.

Kangaroos and their relatives

Kangaroos, wallabies, pademelons and potoroos belong to a large group of marsupials commonly called *macropods*, which means "big-feet". The easiest way for a macropod to cover long distances or move quickly is to hop. Their legs are very muscular and powerful and, as they hop, their long feet and legs make them look as if they are "spring-loaded".

A macropod's tail is strong and heavy. It provides extra weight at the back of the animal to balance out the weight at the front, so macropods don't topple over while they are hopping!

How long, how high and how fast?

A macropod's "spring" comes from an elastic *tendon* in each leg that joins the leg bone to the long foot. As the kangaroo lands on the ground the tendon stretches and becomes longer. Then, like a giant rubber band, it bounces back, or contracts, to its shorter size. This tendon action helps power the macropod's jump and has enabled some pretty impressive records to be set.

	Kangaroo	Human
Longest leap	12.8 metres	8.95 metres
Highest jump	3.1 metres	2.45 metres
Fastest speed	64 kilometres an hour	37 kilometres an hour

Mareeba rock-wallaby (*left*) and red kangaroo (*right*) compared to the size of a man.

Small and large macropods

Although all macropods have big feet, all differ in size, habitat and diet. Larger macropods, like kangaroos, usually live together in small groups, or in larger families called *mobs*. Smaller macropods often live alone in areas where there is a lot of shelter and it is easier to escape or hide from predators.

Phylum: Chordata
Class: Mammalia

The colour of the allied rock-wallaby's fur matches its rocky home.

Above: The long-nosed potoroo looks a little like a bandicoot.

Small animals with big feet

Wallabies, pademelons, bettongs, potoroos and quokkas are smaller than kangaroos, and, like their bigger relatives, females have a pouch that opens at the top. Most live close to grassy woodlands or forests where they can quickly and easily find shelter and plenty of grass, leaves, fruits or leaves to eat. Rock-wallabies live along cliffs and hide in groups of rocks. They have special padded feet that absorb shock and stop them from falling off the wet or slippery surfaces as they jump.

Red-necked pademelons live in and around the edges of forests.

Endangered small macropods

The bridled nailtail wallaby was once common in the central parts of Queensland, New South Wales and Victoria. In the 1930s it was thought to be extinct until a very small group was rediscovered in Queensland in 1973. Today its numbers are still very low. Small macropods are often eaten by dingoes, feral foxes and feral cats and many of their habitats have been replaced by large, cleared paddocks. For some small macropods, captive breeding and release programs are needed to keep their numbers stable.

A bridled nailtail wallaby.

A burrowing bettong.

A brush-tailed bettong, or woylie.

Lumholtz's tree-kangaroo is very shy.

Tree-kangaroos

Shy, secretive tree-kangaroos live high in the tops of rain-forest trees where they feed upon leaves and forest fruits at night. Their powerful arms are shorter and stronger than the arms of other kangaroos, and they have very sharp claws to help them climb. The tree-kangaroo is the only kangaroo that can move its back legs one at a time to "walk" along a branch. They can even walk backwards!

Above: Large male red kangaroos can grow as tall as a man.
Right: The common wallaroo, sometimes called the euro, lives alone.
Below: Eastern grey kangaroos feed during the late afternoon and early morning.

The larger kangaroos

The largest macropods are kangaroos and the red kangaroo is the largest hopping mammal in the world. Kangaroos live together in groups known as mobs, which are led by the strongest males. Kangaroos are *crepuscular*, which means they feed at dawn and dusk and spend the hottest parts of the day resting in the shade. Wallaroos are smaller than kangaroos, but larger than wallabies. Unlike most kangaroos and wallabies, wallaroos don't live in a mob. They live alone among rocky cliffs and hills.

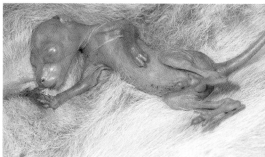

Above: In the pouch, joeys drink milk and learn to nibble grass. *Top right:* An eastern grey kangaroo joey stays in its mother's pouch until it is eleven months old.

A tiny baby joey has developed back legs, arms and tail, but has not yet formed eyes, ears or fur.

Out and about

It takes about a year before a joey leaves the pouch for good, but once it does it still stays close to its mother for protection. Even when it begins eating grass, a joey will still sometimes poke its head back into the pouch for a drink. By this time, its mother probably already has another furless, undeveloped pink "jelly bean" joey drinking milk from a different nipple.

Tucked away

When a kangaroo joey is born, it is the size and colour of a pink jelly bean. After it has struggled its way into the safety and warmth of the pouch, it attaches to one of its mother's four teats, which swells inside the joey's mouth to make sure it stays attached and has a constant supply of milk. Joeys don't begin to leave the pouch until they are fully-furred, at about nine months of age.

Placental mammals
Giving birth to fully formed young

Baby placental mammals spend a lot of time developing inside their mother's tummy before they are born. Inside the mother, they are fed, protected, and receive oxygen from a large bag called a *placenta*. When the baby is born, the mother's body also pushes out the placenta, which at this stage is known as "afterbirth".

By the time they are born, most baby placental mammals have a body covering of fur, or hair, and have well-formed arms, legs, tails, wings or flippers. They drink their mother's milk and she spends a lot of time looking after them as they grow. Most placental mammals are diurnal, which means they are active during the daytime. Humans are placental mammals.

Dingoes

Dingoes are naturally thin wild dogs and are Australia's largest meat-eating mammals. Purebred dingoes have four white paws and a white tip on the end of the tail. The most common colour is sandy-yellow or tan, but some may be black and others creamy-white.

Dingo pups stop drinking their mother's milk after 3–4 months.

Phylum: Chordata
Class: Mammalia

Bats and flying-foxes

There are two different groups of bats — megabats, which are "mega" or large, and microbats which are "micro" or small. Flying-foxes are megabats that feed on fruit and plant juices and give birth to furry young. Microbats are also called *insectivorous* bats because they are nocturnal insect hunters. Newborn microbats don't have any fur.

Black flying-fox

Native rats and mice

Rats and mice are rodents and there are over 60 different types, or species, of rodents living in Australia. There are more rodents in the world than any other type of mammal! This is because many rodents are able to give birth to a few litters every breeding season.

Cape York melomys

Dolphins, whales and dugongs

These marine mammals give birth to their babies underwater! Like all mammals, they breathe air to survive, so after a calf is born it must reach the surface quickly to take its first breath.

Bottlenose dolphin

Fur-seals and sea-lions

Spending their lives both on land and in the water, these placental mammals give birth to one baby at a time, called a pup. Pups are born on land and while they are still drinking their mother's milk they stay among the colony when their mothers head out to sea to hunt.

New Zealand fur-seals

Hanging around

Bats and flying-foxes

Bats have wings and can fly, so sometimes they almost look like a bird. But, bats are covered in fur, not feathers, which makes them mammals! In fact, bats and flying-foxes are the only mammals that can truly fly. Their long fingers are joined to their back legs by a thin, stretchy skin that forms their wings.

Bats are nocturnal, so they hunt or search for food at night. During the day, hundreds of thousands of bats "hang out" together, upside down as they roost in a large group known as a colony or camp.

The diadem leafnosed-bat waits to catch its prey by surprise.

Blind as a bat?

Actually, bats are not blind! Some insect-eating microbats have very small eyes, but they can still see! Bats simply don't need good eyesight because it's not important when finding prey. Instead, microbats make sounds that are so high pitched they can't be heard by humans. These sounds travel away from the bat like invisible ripples in the air. When they hit an object, they reflect, or "echo" back. The patterns of the "echoed" sounds help the bats work out exactly where, and how far away, their prey is, even in total darkness!

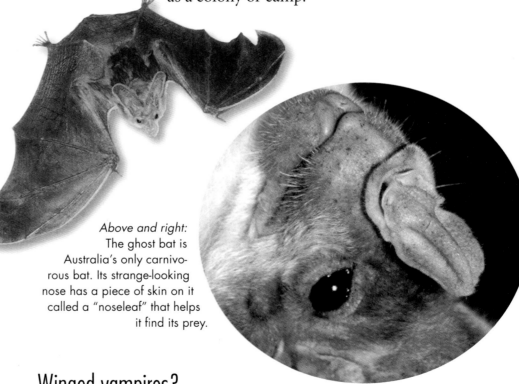

Above and right:
The ghost bat is Australia's only carnivorous bat. Its strange-looking nose has a piece of skin on it called a "noseleaf" that helps it find its prey.

Winged vampires?

A ghost bat swoops down on its prey, wraps it in its wings and kills it with bites from its sharp teeth. They are not blood-suckers, but they are carnivorous hunters of birds, lizards, large insects, frogs and other mammals, including other bats.

Phylum: Chordata
Class: Mammalia

50

Upside-down living

During the day, flying-foxes hang upside down as they roost in a large and noisy colony, called a camp. They sleep, fan their wings to stay cool, groom their fur, and even give birth while hanging upside down! There may be thousands of bats in the camp, but a mother can easily find her baby simply by its smell and its call.

Right: A flying-fox colony.

Spectacled flying-foxes "camp" in a paperbark tree.

Helping the bush

Many eucalypt and rainforest trees rely on flying foxes to spread pollen, which sticks to the bats' fur from flower to flower and takes seeds from one area of the forest to another. A flying-fox can travel up to 100 kilometres a night from its camp to a feeding spot that the group finds by smell and sight. While hanging upside-down, a bat bites off a small piece of ripe fruit, squishes it between the roof of its mouth and tongue, and swallows any juice and small seeds. The pulp is spat out onto the ground below. Any seeds pass out with the bat's droppings and land on the ground, ready to grow a new tree.

Flying-foxes wrap their wings around their body like a blanket.

Respectable rodents
Australia's native rats and mice

The spinifex hopping-mouse lives in the desert.

Living space

Most rodents are nocturnal. They live in many different habitats and make their nests on the ground, in trees and hollows, and in even creek banks. Desert rodents spend the day in an underground burrow.

Amazingly, rodents make up more than half the total number of mammals on Earth! Most rodents are small, but the largest rodent in the world, the South American capybara, can weigh 50 kilograms! One of Australia's largest rodents, the black-footed tree-rat, weighs just 1 kilogram.

Australia's native rodents don't carry nasty diseases like rats brought into Australia from other countries can. Native rats and mice spend a lot of time washing and wiping their fur to keep themselves nice and clean.

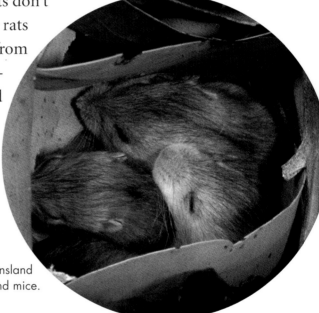

Right: Baby Queensland pebble-mound mice.

A greater stick-nest rat.

Endangered rat

The greater stick-nest rat is now found only on three tiny islands off Australia's southern coast. It builds huge nests out of sticks and branches, which it bites off the tree and carries in its teeth.

An important link in the food chain

Rodents are very important to the food chain. They are one of the biggest sources of food for larger predators such as birds and snakes.

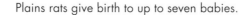
Plains rats give birth to up to seven babies.

Phylum: Chordata
Class: Mammalia

The prehensile-tailed rat climbs in trees and wraps its tail around branches to help it climb safely.

Wear and tear

Like wombats' teeth, rodents' teeth don't fall out. But they never become too long because they are worn down when rodents gnaw on seeds, grasses, leaves, fruit, insects and animals.

Waterproof fur

Water-rats and platypuses are land mammals that spend part of their lives in the water. The water-rat's thick fur is waterproof. Its back feet are webbed and are used like underwater paddles to help it swim. Its long tail can be used as a rudder to help the rat steer through the water as it hunts. Although they mostly live in freshwater, water-rats can also live in saltwater, and in some places, even down by the beach!

Water-rats will even eat freshwater crayfish!

Dingoes howl but don't bark.

Dingoes

The dingo, Australia's only native dog, is a distant relative of the Asian wolf. Dingoes were brought to Australia by boat around 5000 years ago, as the pets of Asian fishing and trading people. These naturally thin hunters are now found in every mainland State and in most habitats across Australia.

Dingoes live in a group of up to twelve members known as a "pack". The pack is usually led by a male and female pair and the female gives birth to pups once a year. Pups from earlier litters make up the rest of the pack.

Dingo talk

Dingoes may look like dogs, but they don't bark like dogs — instead, dingoes howl. Howling is how dingoes talk to other members of their pack.

Sometimes pack members fight over food.

Skilled hunters

Dingoes are Australia's largest carnivores. They use their excellent senses of sight, smell and hearing to find prey. When hunting small animals such as lizards, rodents and rabbits, a dingo will usually hunt alone. To bring down large animals like the red kangaroo, dingoes must work as a pack.

A dead wallaby is a good meal for a dingo.

Phylum: Chordata
Class: Mammalia

Above: Fraser Island in Queensland is home to many purebred dingoes.

A litter of little dingoes

Like domestic dogs, dingoes give birth to a number of pups known as a *litter*. When they are born, the pups are helpless, blind and too weak to walk. It takes about ten days for the pups to open their eyes, but it takes them less than an hour to sniff out their mother's teats and begin to drink her milk!

Dingo-free State

Six hundred years ago, Tasmanian devils lived on mainland Australia. Today they survive only in Tasmania where there are no dingoes. Dingoes probably out-hunted the devils for food and even hunted the devils as prey!

Below: Six dingo pups wait for their mother to return from a hunting trip.

Ocean life

Bottlenose dolphins always seem to smile.

Dolphins, whales & dugongs

Mammals don't just live on land, they also live in the ocean. Dolphins, whales and dugongs, as well as fur-seals and sea-lions, are all mammals. Dolphins have smooth, torpedo-shaped bodies and excellent eyesight for chasing fish underwater. Several types of whales visit Australian waters, and dugongs cruise the calm coastal waters looking for meadows of seagrass to eat.

Life as a dolphin

Dolphins live in family groups called *pods*. A dolphin's tail, called a "fluke", works like a powerful paddle helping playful dolphins swim quickly, surf waves and leap up to 6 metres out of the water!

Dolphins, whales and dugongs spend their entire lives in the water. Females give birth to a calf close to the surface and steer it upwards to take its first breath.

Having a whale of a time

Like dolphins, whales breathe through a blowhole on the top of the head. They also have a "fluke" tail, which helps them leap headfirst out of the water in a playful act called *breaching*.

A dugong and calf.

Sea cows

The dugong is also known as a sea cow. It is a marine mammal that eats seagrass, rather than fish. Dugongs are endangered, so it is important to protect the seagrass beds where they feed.

Scientists are not sure why whales breach, it may be just that they are just playing.

Phylum: Chordata
Class: Mammalia

Above: New Zealand fur-seals also live and hunt in Australia.
Left: A female Australian sea-lion.

Fur-seals and sea-lions

Fur-seals and sea-lions are ocean carnivores that hunt fish and squid. Unlike other marine mammals, seals and sea-lions do come out of the ocean. They hunt in the sea, but live and give birth to their pups on land.

Teeth and whiskers

Seals and sea-lions have large meat-eating teeth similar to other mammal carnivores such as the dingo. They need these sharp teeth to grip hold of slippery fish and squid. They also have very long, sensitive whiskers that can detect tiny changes in water movement. These whiskers help the seal hunt in dark water, because although the seal may not be able to see a fish, it can tell exactly where the fish is by the movement of the water.

Cold water hunters

While swimming and hunting, seals and sea-lions use their front flippers to propel them quickly through the water. To keep them warm and dry in their chilly hunting grounds, they have a thick layer of fat, or blubber, and three layers of oily, water-proof fur.

Which pup?

After a few days hunting at sea, mother fur-seals return to the colony on the beach where hundreds of pups are calling loudly, trying to find their mothers. Amazingly, it doesn't take long for a mother seal to find the right pup, firstly by sound and then, smell.

A New Zealand fur-seal with her pup.

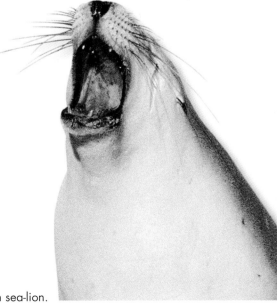

An Australian sea-lion.

Birds
Feathered fliers

If the body of an animal is covered in feathers, it must be a bird! Feathers set birds apart from all other animals. Birds are vertebrates because they have a backbone, but to have babies birds lay eggs. They are warm-blooded and have scales covering their feet and legs. Although all birds have wings, not all birds can fly!

Australia is home to over 800 different types of bird. High in the sky, in the trees, in the bushes, on the ground, in the city and out on the ocean, even underground — almost everywhere you look you will probably see them. If you stop and listen you may hear their calls, whistles, screeches, barks or songs.

Left: The black-necked stork is often called a jabiru.
Below: Egrets during a feeding frenzy.

Phylum: CHORDATA
Class: Aves

Passerines — perching songbirds

More than half of all of the birds in Australia belong to a group known as *passerines*. They are also called "perching songbirds", because they use their special perching feet to grip on to a branch and because they sing loudly. Their songs are often long and made up of high notes, long notes, and many different sounds and melodies. Australia is home to the world's biggest perching songbird, the superb lyrebird, which has some of the most amazing songs and sounds of all.

Rainbow
bee-eater

Magpie

Non-passerines

The rest of Australia's birds belong to the group known as *non-passerines*. These birds don't have special perching toes and can't sing long, loud or difficult songs. Their legs, feet and toes come in all shapes and sizes, depending on where the bird lives and how it searches for its food.

Female Australasian
shoveler

Common bronzewing

Australian pelican

Superb lyrebird

Naked necks

An emu has very few feathers on its neck and head and the cassowary has none at all! Both have bright blue neck skin.

The emu and cassowary

Australia's largest birds, the emu and the cassowary, belong to a group of birds called *ratites*, which cannot fly. Ratites may be large, but they have extremely small wings. The shape of their feathers makes these flightless birds look "hairy".

The large legs and feet of flightless birds are strong and built for running. Cassowaries live in the rainforest, while emus wander the open plains. To lay eggs, both birds scratch a shallow "nest" on the ground.

Wandering the land

Groups of emus may walk hundreds of kilometres across the plains, picking at insects, native flowers, seeds, leaves and different types of grass. The emu is Australia's largest bird and grows up to 2 metres tall. Emus have long legs and can run very fast, reaching speeds of almost 50 kilometres an hour!

Emus are omnivores because they eat both plants and animals.

Phylum: Chordata
Class: Aves

60

Male southern cassowaries look after the chicks once they hatch.

The fruit of the blue quandong tree is a favourite food for cassowaries.

Doting dads

Baby cassowaries and baby emus are born with brown stripes that disappear at around three months of age. The chicks are cared for and taken on feeding trips by their fathers. Mother emus and cassowaries lay the large green eggs, but they don't help look after the eggs or the chicks.

One big gulp

A cassowary can swallow food the size of an orange, whole! Because they are omnivores they eat almost anything, including snails, fungi, fruit and seeds — even dead rats and birds!

The two red flaps of skin that dangle from the neck of the cassowary are called "wattles".

Diving fisherbirds

Cormorants, darters and pelicans

Because of its S-shaped neck, a darter is sometimes called a snake-bird.

Even though these birds spend much of their time swimming and diving, their feathers are not waterproof. Their bodies produce a special oil, which they spread over their feathers when they preen. This helps them keep the water out for a little while before the oil washes off.

Cormorants, darters and pelicans are all fish hunters and the shape of their beak tells you how each bird catches its slippery meal. Cormorants have a hooked bill used to grasp fish. Darters have a sharp, pointed bill for spearing fish. Pelicans have an enormous sack-like pouch which they use to scoop up fish for their dinner.

Australia's largest cormorant, the great cormorant, drying its wings.

Propelled by paddles

Diving birds have large webbed feet that work together like a single flipper to help propel them swiftly underwater as they hunt for food. The stiff tail feathers and wings of darters and cormorants also help them balance as they dive. Some diving birds can stay underwater for up to 40 seconds.

Hung out to dry

Because their feathers aren't waterproof, after a long time in the water, cormorants and darters become "water-logged" and their feathers get very heavy. They must then go and sit in the sun with their wings spread out to dry them.

Phylum: Chordata
Class: Aves

Flying high

Pelicans are large, heavy birds, but that doesn't stop them being wonderful fliers! Like all birds, their bones are hollow and very light. Their 2.5-metre wingspan and finger-like wing tips help them soar to heights of 3000 metres on rising currents of warm air known as *thermals*. By gliding from thermal to thermal, pelicans don't need to flap their wings very often, so they don't tire easily and can stay in the air for up to 24 hours and travel hundreds of kilometres a day!

Team work

A flock of pelicans works together to "herd" a school of fish into the shallows. Using their long bills like underwater sticks and beating their wings on the water's surface, the pelicans gradually move the fish into a tight group where it is easier to catch many in one big mouthful.

Filling the bill

A pelican's bill can be up to 50 centimetres long — the longest of any bird in the world! The stretchy pouch is used to scoop up prey and up to 13 litres of water! Pelicans get rid of the water by squashing the bill pouch against their chest. Any fish are trapped and moved around until they can be swallowed headfirst and whole. Sometimes pelicans scoop up frogs, tadpoles, shrimps, even turtles! This one (*left*) has an octopus.

A straw-necked ibis.

Spoonbills, ibises and storks

With their lanky legs and large bills, these birds wade through water, wetlands and across mudflats as they stalk their prey. Their long toes are not webbed, but are spread wide apart which helps them walk easily across muddy surfaces without sinking in too deep.

Each bird's bill is shaped to suit the way it searches for food. Storks and ibises have long, strong bills able to probe deep into swampy ground. Spoonbills keep their bill in the water and sweep their head from side to side. When they touch prey, they snap the bill tightly shut.

A pair of nesting yellow-billed spoonbills.

Sacred ibises roosting.

Farmer's friends

Ibises feed naturally on fresh-water yabbies, mussels, fish, frogs and snakes. Sometimes, too many ibises gather near cities, where they eat scraps humans leave behind instead of their natural diet. Farmers like ibises because they protect crops by eating leaf-munching grasshoppers.

Fighting feet

When nesting, spoonbills build a sturdy platform of sticks, sometimes as high as 20 metres above the water. Male spoonbills become aggressive and defend the nest if another male comes too close. They snap their bills, flap their wings and lunge at each other with their legs and feet, like a pair of roosters fighting.

Phylum: Chordata
Class: Aves

64

The black-necked stork's long bill helps it to grab prey in its wetland habitat.

Newly hatched black-necked storks have soft, down-covered bodies.

Stately storks

The black-necked stork is also known as the jabiru and is the only stork that lives in Australia. They live around wetlands and billabongs, where they poke their beaks into swampy ground and stalk through the water looking for reptiles, frogs, crabs and water-rats to eat. A stork's chicks don't all hatch at the same time. In fact, only one chick hatches per day! Ibises and spoonbills also space out their chicks in this way.

Black-necked storks have bright red legs.

These immature black-necked storks are more than three months old.

The rufous heron is also called the nankeen night heron.

Sharp-eyed hunters

Herons and egrets

These birds live in flocks of thousands and roost in trees and bushes near creeks and rivers. They are very patient hunters and will wait, watch, then stalk their prey as they wade silently through their watery habitats.

Herons and egrets are very graceful to watch. They stand like a statue in the one spot, waiting for the right moment to lunge forward and snatch up passing prey. During breeding season, both males and females grow long, lace-like feathers along their back and chest to help attract a mate.

Lone night-stalker

The rufous heron is the only heron that hunts at night. During the day, hundreds of them roost together, hiding among the branches and leaves of trees close to the water.

Two cattle egrets prepare to mate.

Nesting and resting

When they're not out hunting, cattle egrets often share the trees with thousands of other egrets and herons. The male cattle egret's job is to look after his nest and attract a female. He ruffles his lacy back feathers, flaps his wings and even waves a stick in his bill trying to attract the attention of a female cattle egret.

The striated heron hunts during the day.

Phylum: Chordata
Class: Aves

A pied heron preens its grey and white feathers.

A cattle egret stretches out one wing.

Intermediate egrets stalk fishes, insects, crayfish and frogs.

Expert hunters

The sharply pointed bill of herons and egrets is often used as a spear for stabbing prey. A special, flexible joint between two bones, or *vertebrae*, in the neck allows them to dart their bill into the water and strike at their prey with amazing speed. Their bill is also used to snap at prey and grab hold of it like a fine pair of tweezers.

The fierce wedge-tailed eagle.

Ruling the skies
Eagles, ospreys and falcons

Carnivores of the sky, these diurnal, or daytime-hunting birds are known as "raptors". Raptors are powerful birds that seize their prey with their sharp claws, called talons, and carry it away. They use strong, hooked beaks to rip and tear their prey into smaller pieces.

Like most predators, raptors have forward-facing eyes. They have excellent eyesight and can see the detail on distant animals much more clearly than humans can.

King predator

With a wingspan of about 2.5 metres, the mighty wedge-tailed eagle is Australia's largest bird of prey. It can seize and carry away animals the size of a small kangaroo!

Ospreys nest up to 30 metres above the ground.

Peregrine falcon

The fastest of them all

The peregrine falcon is the fastest flying bird in the world and is a supreme hunter. As it stoops, or dives through the air, it reaches speeds of up to 140 kilometres an hour!

Bonding and breeding

Raptors are large birds, so they have to build large nests. An osprey's nest of sticks and twigs can be huge! Each year the nest is "renovated" or expanded by adding more and more sticks. Many raptors mate for life and the female sits on the eggs or guards the chicks while the male hunts for food to bring back to the nest. When the chicks are old enough to be left alone, the female also goes out hunting.

Phylum: Chordata
Class: Aves

Above: An osprey must stay on the lookout for other birds that might steal its catch.
Left: White-bellied sea-eagle.

Gone fishing

White-bellied sea-eagles and ospreys are excellent fishers. As they soar above the ocean their keen eyes spot fish swimming just below the surface. They swoop down to snatch their unwary prey and take it back to a perch to eat. They have sharp bumps called *spicules* underneath their feet to help them hold their slippery prize. Both ospreys and white-bellied sea-eagles catch sea snakes and have thick, scaly skin on their feet and legs to protect them from the venomous fangs.

Webbed waddlers

Ducks

On land, ducks look quite awkward because they waddle when they walk. In the water, however, it's a different story! A duck's webbed feet work like paddles and propel them quickly and smoothly through the water as they swim.

There aren't any nerves or blood vessels in a duck's feet, so ducks can't feel the cold water! Their warm covering of thick, waterproof feathers, allows them to swim on icy cold lakes, ponds or rivers without getting frost-bite or even shivering.

A plumed whistling-duck.

Roosting together

During the day, ducks huddle together in groups for protection. They travel at night to feed, mainly on grass, water weeds and seeds, but sometimes on insects.

Pacific black duck

Taking a bath

Ducks keep themselves nice and clean by preening and shaking their feathers when they bathe and wash.

The bill of a male freckled duck becomes more colourful during breeding season.

A rare beauty

The freckled duck is one of the rarest waterbirds in the world and is only found in Australia! During the breeding season, the males are easy to spot because they get a patch of bright red skin on top of their bills.

Phylum: Chordata
Class: Aves

Australian shelducks at rest on a large, grassy platform.

Nests are lined with soft down.

Where to nest

Ducks have many different types of nests and nesting spots, from bowl-shaped nests of twigs by the water's edge, to shallow grass-lined nests on the ground — they even nest in large hollow trees. When she is ready to lay her eggs, a female duck lines the nest with soft "down" feathers that she plucks from her chest.

Dabbling duckling patrol

Female pacific black ducks usually lay up to ten eggs. All of the eggs hatch at once and the chicks begin to leave the nest to feed when they are just one day old! Of course, this keeps mother duck very busy. She must stay close and keep careful watch over her ducklings while they learn to "dabble", or search for food with their "heads-down, tails-up".

A pacific black duck and duckling.

Magpie goose

Flocking together

Geese and swans

Noisy honks, grunts and trumpets are the sounds made by geese and swans. Like ducks, they spend most of their time in the water and belong to a group of birds called "waterfowl".

Waterfowls' different-shaped beaks are suited to the food they eat. Magpie geese have strong, hooked bills to dig out the roots of water plants. Cape Barren geese have short bills for grazing on grass and seeds. A swan's beak has a small hook on the end. They nibble weeds growing on top of the water and also pluck plants from below the surface.

Lanky legs

The legs and toes of a magpie goose are long and their feet are only half webbed. This helps them to walk easily through swampy, muddy wetlands as they search for food.

A Cape Barren goose with its young.

Gosling groups

Geese and swans are very protective of their young both before and after they hatch, but when Cape Barren goslings reach six weeks old, they are left to look after themselves. Up to 50 goslings live together and as soon as they can fly they join a larger flock and move from feeding ground to feeding ground.

Baby swans, like these black swans, are called cygnets.

Phylum: Chordata
Class: Aves

A mother magpie goose keeps her goslings close.

Each magpie goose has a hard bumpy bone on its head and the larger the bump, the older the bird.

In their thousands

When plenty of food is available, it is not unusual for a few thousand magpie geese to flock together in one large group. Imagine the noise of a few thousand "honkers" in the one area!

Mound builders

Brush-turkey and mallee fowl

Australian brush-turkey

Amazing chicks

Once they hatch from their eggs, brush-turkey chicks tunnel their way up to the surface, climb out of the mound and sprint away. They are already fully covered in feathers, so young brush-turkeys can fly just a few hours after hatching!

They may spend most of their time running or walking along the ground, but Australian brush-turkeys and mallee fowl can fly when they need to escape predators or reach low branches to roost. They belong to the group of birds called "megapodes", which means "big feet".

Using their powerful feet, males busily scratch and flick soil, leaves and twigs into a huge nesting mound where the female lays her eggs. As the buried leaves and twigs begin to rot, the inside of the mound starts to warm up. The male makes sure that the mound stays at the right temperature for the eggs to develop and hatch.

Above: Male mallee fowls must make sure the mound temperature is just right.
Left: The mallee is a dry, sandy habitat.

Built-in thermometer

How does a male know whether the mound's temperature is right? He has a built-in thermometer — his beak, which he pokes into the mound! Between 32–34 degrees Celsius is the best temperature for the eggs to hatch. If the mound is getting too hot, he scratches dirt and sticks away. If it begins to cool down, he flicks leaves and dirt on top.

Phylum: Chordata
Class: Aves

74

Waders and walkers

Jacana, bustard and crane

Long legs, long necks and long bills help cranes and jacanas spend much of their lives on watery ground, either wading or walking in search of food. The Australian bustard, which lives on dry, open plains, also shares these features, but with one difference...

...rather than having three long, slender toes facing forwards and one pointing backwards, the bustard doesn't have a back toe. Its feet are suited to running and walking, not wading.

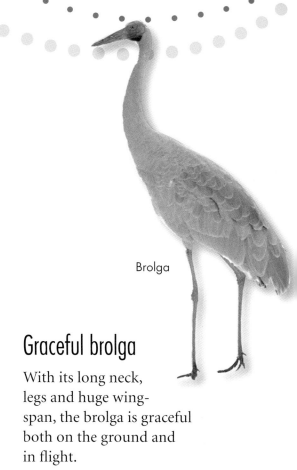

Brolga

Graceful brolga

With its long neck, legs and huge wing-span, the brolga is graceful both on the ground and in flight.

Australian bustards crouch down low to hide if they are frightened.

Crouching for cover

The Australian bustard stands about a metre tall as it wanders the plains in search of food. If threatened by an intruder or predator, it quickly crouches down. The patterns on its feathers help it blend in with the colours and patterns on the ground.

A comb-crested jacana and its eggs.

Eggs afloat

Male jacanas build a floating nest of reeds and grasses on top of other water plants. Once the female has laid her eggs, the male and female take turns sitting on them until they hatch.

Coastal living

Plovers, waders, gulls & relatives

The red-necked avocet has a long, thin, upturned bill.

Most members of this group of birds live along coastal shores, wetlands, mudflats and reefs, where they roost, nest, wade and search for food on the ground. Some species of wading birds also live inland, far from the ocean.

For many of these birds, building a nest is easy. It is usually a very simple bed of sticks or a shallow hole scratched in the ground. Sometimes they line the nest with trampled grass or leaves, but most often the eggs are laid straight onto the sand, shells, rocks or dirt.

Upturned avocets

Avocets differ from their long-legged relatives, the stilts, because their beaks curve upwards. As they wade or swim, they pick at small animals in the mud or on the water's surface.

A beach stone-curlew on nest duty.

Red-capped plovers lay their eggs on the ground.

Stone-curlews

Beach and bush stone-curlews live where their names suggest, but the bush stone-curlew also lives by the coast. These fast-running nocturnal hunters are also known as "thick-knees".

Plovers and dotterels

Dotterels and plovers are beach birds that dash around searching for small crabs, beach worms and bivalves, such as pipis, to eat. When nesting, these birds, use "bluff" to protect their eggs. If a predator approaches, the adult moves away from the nest, flapping its wings and pretending it can't fly. This tricks the predator and lures it away from the precious eggs.

Phylum: Chordata
Class: Aves

Crested terns live all along Australia's coastline.

Gulls and terns

Fish and crabs are the natural diet of gulls and terns, but these birds are also great scavengers of scraps left by humans. As terns fly, they snatch insects from the air or swoop down to grab small fish from below the water's surface.

Oystercatchers

An oystercatcher's bright red beak makes it one of the most recognisable shore birds. As they feed their young, adult oystercatchers also teach them what to eat, where to find it, and how to get it out of the shell.

A pied oystercatcher uses its strong bill to prise open a pipi.

Bright and bold
Cockatoos and parrots

Early settlers once called Australia "Parrot Land" for a very good reason. There are 53 different types of these bright and beautiful feathered fliers living on this continent, and 44 of them are found nowhere else in the world!

Parrots use their strong, curved beaks to crack open the hard shell of seeds and get to the vitamin-packed kernel inside. Their "handy" feet allow them to hold food and move it around because their toes are *zygodactylous*, which means that two toes point forwards and two point backwards.

Left, top to bottom: Male gang-gang cockatoo; Major Mitchell's cockatoo and Sulphur-crested cockatoos. *Above and right:* Galahs often pair for life.

What's up cocky?

A cockatoo has a crest of feathers on top of its head that can be raised when the bird is excited or frightened. Crests may be long or short, brightly coloured or plain. The vibrant crest of Australia's most familiar parrot, the sulphur-crested cockatoo, is bright yellow.

Phylum: Chordata
Class: Aves

Home in a hollow

Parrots and cockatoos don't build nests. Instead, they sleep and lay their eggs in holes, called hollows, which form in the trunks and branches of old trees. It may take hundreds of years before a tree reaches an age where it begins to hollow out. Some parrots use the same hollow year after year. Using their strong bills, they scrape wood from the inside walls of the hollow to use as a soft covering on which to lay their eggs. Hollows provide homes for many animals, which makes it extra important to look after big, old trees.

Left: A male eclectus parrot (green) feeds the female (red and blue) while she stays in the hollow protecting her eggs from predators.
Right: Budgerigars are naturally green.

Above: Mallee ringneck parrots nest in hollows near freshwater creeks, billabongs or dams.

Barking owl

Silent night stalkers

Owls and frogmouths

Rather than being built for speed, these night-time hunters are built for silence. Their feathers are very soft and "pat" the air like a soft tissue, so they hardly make a sound. What they lose in speed, they gain in stealth because they are able to sneak up on their prey to take it by surprise!

The eyes of owls and frogmouths are huge and take up most of the room inside the skull. This leaves just enough room for a tiny, pea-sized brain, but no room at all for any muscles to attach to their eyeballs. For this reason, they cannot "roll" their eyes or move them inside their heads like humans can. Instead, owls must turn their head if they need to look to the side or behind them.

An owl that "barks"

"Wook-wook" is the sound that gives the barking owl its name. It hunts at night for reptiles, small mammals and other nocturnal birds and insects, but can sometimes be seen out hunting before the sun goes down.

Is a frogmouth an owl?

No! Frogmouths are not owls. Owls have long, sharp claws, called talons to grab and puncture their prey. They also have a sharp beak to tear their meal to pieces. Frogmouths have short claws for scratching leaves and a big, wide, "frog-like" mouth. They gulp their prey down and swallow it whole.

Left: Frogs are a favourite food of the tawny frog-mouth.

Master of camouflage

The feathers of the tawny frog-mouth look just like the bark of a tree! If it wants to hide, it looks up into the sky, closes its eyes and stiffens its body. The spiky feathers on top of its beak help it resemble a broken branch.

The tawny frogmouth is not an owl.

Phylum: Chordata
Class: Aves

This southern boobook owl has caught an insect in flight.

The lesser sooty owl lives in northern rainforests.

"Catching" sounds

Owls have excellent eyesight, but their sense of hearing is also very important. Some owls have a face shaped like a shallow dish, which helps them "catch" sounds and makes their hearing even better. We can also "catch" sounds by cupping our hands behind our ears. Hearing is often more important to owls than seeing because they need to pinpoint exactly where their prey is in pitch darkness.

Life on the farm

The barn owl is a farmer's friend. It makes its home in the roof or rafters of barns where it sleeps during the day. At night it comes out to feed on mice and rats, which eat the farmer's grain.

Barn owl

Kingfishers, bee-eaters and dollarbirds

Forest kingfisher

Kingfishers

Kingfishers use their strong bills to catch small reptiles, frogs, insects and spiders. Those that live by the water also hunt for fishes, crabs and yabbies. Kookaburras are the largest of the kingfisher family.

From high on their perch, these birds use their excellent eyesight to spot small animals moving below. They swoop down and pounce on their prey or pluck it from the water. While flying, they use their strong beaks and good timing to snatch insects from the air.

Holding prey tightly in its beak, a kingfisher, bee-eater or dollarbird may bang it on the ground or against a perch, which helps soften the animal and makes it easier to swallow.

Bee-eaters

There is only one type of bee-eater in Australia, the beautifully coloured rainbow bee-eater. Bee-eaters sit on a high branch and keep watch for their favourite foods — bees and wasps. They take their prey back to their perch and rub its body along the branch to remove the sting from the end of a bee or wasp's tail.

Dollarbirds

Dollarbirds visit Australia every summer to breed. As they fly, a round patch of pale blue feathers can be seen on their wings. This patch is the shape and size of a one-dollar coin which is how the dollarbird got its name.

Dollarbirds are expert insect catchers.

A rainbow bee-eater may catch and eat more than 100 bees a day!

Phylum: Chordata
Class: Aves

Above: The blue-winged kookaburra lives across northern Australia. *Inset:* The laughing kookaburra is the largest of the kingfishers.

Newly hatched blue-winged kookaburra chicks are bald.

Blue-winged kookaburra chicks almost ready for take-off.

Everyone pitches in

When they hatch, baby kookaburras are blind, bald and completely helpless. They must be protected and fed by their parents and older brothers and sisters until they learn to fly for themselves.

Baby food

Until they are able to hunt for themselves, baby kookaburras grow big and strong on a diet of small lizards, insects, snakes and mice.

Singing for a living

A willie wagtail.

Passerines – perching songbirds

Being able to chirp, sing, whistle and call is what makes passerines, or perching birds, the most widespread group of birds in the world. People once believed that when birds burst into song in the morning they were singing to welcome the rising sun, but in fact this is how birds communicate with each other.

Songbirds have a very musclar voicebox, called a *syrinx*, that allows them to sing long, loud and complicated songs. In the early morning and late afternoon, a male sings loudly to let other males know the boundaries of his territory.

Wee willie wagtail

Willie wagtails run and hop along the ground, stopping to wag their tails from side to side, before flying in a low, zig-zag pattern chasing after insects. Their chirp almost sounds as if they are saying "sweet, sweet little creature".

The pretty variegated fairy-wren.

Dainty fairies

Pretty little fairy-wrens have long tails, which stick up in the air when they perch. They live in small groups and search for seeds or hunt insects.

The metallic starling is Australia's only native starling.

Bend and grip

Each foot of a perching bird has three toes that point forwards and one toe that points backwards. When the bird lands and crouches down on a branch or twig, its toes curl around and "lock" it onto the perch so it can't fall off. To release their grip they simply straighten their legs.

Phylum: Chordata
Class: Aves

Male figbirds call out loudly to tell other males to stay out of their territory.

Green catbirds also call to mark their territory.

Noisy pittas are often heard, but rarely seen as they hop along the forest floor looking for food.

A pied butcherbird perched on a branch.

Supreme songsters

The sounds of the forests and bushlands just wouldn't be the same without the songs and calls of the catbird, lyrebird, noisy pitta and butcher-bird. The superb lyrebird's call is a non-stop medley of mimicked sounds, animal noises and high and low notes. The catbird's wailing cry sounds like a cat's "me-ow", while the noisy pitta's loud whistle seems to ask the question, "Walk-to-work?" Male and female butcherbirds have lovely songs and often such good timing that when they sing together it almost sounds as if only one bird is singing!

The male superb lyrebird likes to show off, using his beautiful, mimicked songs and his display of tail feathers to attract a female.

Amazing mimicry

The superb lyrebird uses his ability to mimic, or copy, almost any sound to attract a female. Superb lyrebirds copy the clear calls of other birds and mammals and join them together to make one incredible song. They even add in the sounds of chainsaws, barking dogs, car engines and anything else they hear in the environment around them.

How could a female resist this display?

A young bird, or nestling, begs its parents for food by opening its mouth and calling.

Crimson chats run quickly along the ground, picking up insects to take back to their young.

Open wide

Young perching birds don't have any feathers when they first hatch. Just like human babies, they rely on their parents to feed them. Sometimes, their brothers and sisters still live nearby and also help out by bringing food and providing protection.

An eastern yellow robin sits with its two nestlings, which are still unable to fly.

The best nests

Perching birds build very fancy nests. They use many different materials, such as grass, twigs, mud, feathers, and even spider webs! Some even dig their way into the bank of a creek and build a nest at the end of the tunnel!

This red-browed finch has found a feather to add to its nest.

A male golden whistler about to feed his nestling a caterpillar.

Metallic starlings build a dome-shaped nest.

The yellow-bellied sunbird builds a hanging nest of bark, leaves, cobwebs and feathers.

The rufous fantail wraps its cone shaped nest of twigs and straw in cobwebs.

The tooth-billed bowerbird uses large, green leaves to decorate its flat, oval-shaped bower.

The golden bowerbird is the smallest bowerbird but makes the biggest bower.

Above: Male satin bowerbirds collect blue objects to decorate the entrance to their bowers and attract females. *Right:* A female satin bowerbird.

Built to impress

Male bowerbirds build a bower out of sticks or leaves, but a bower is not a nest. It is built and decorated with colour in the hope of attracting passing females. If the female likes the look of the male and also the look of his bower, she may enter and allow him to mate with her.

A male regent bowerbird decorates his bower with leaves, snail shells and yellow flowers.

Female regent bowerbirds look very different to males.

The great bowerbird's bower is up to 100 centimetres long and 45 centimetres tall.

A male great bowerbird decorates his bower with white snail shells.

A New Holland honeyeater searching for nectar on a bottlebrush.

A female yellow-bellied sunbird enjoys the sugary nectar.

The eastern spinebill is a type of honeyeater that has a long bill to poke down into flower tubes in search of nectar.

Nectar-feeding songsters

To help them spread their pollen, flowers produce sweet, honey-like nectar which attracts insects. This sugary liquid also attracts birds known as honeyeaters. Most honey-eaters have curved beaks, which they poke down into the base of a flower to reach the nectar, and long tongues that they flicker in and out. On the end of a honeyeater's tongue may be little "brushes" that soak up the nectar like a sponge. Some honeyeaters can flick their tongue in and out of their beak up to ten times a second! Honeyeaters also eat insects and fruit. Some honeyeaters have short bills and usually eat more insects and fruit than long-billed honeyeaters do.

Gouldian finches have bright colours.

The double-barred finch has a white face with a dark rim around it.

The star finch has little white "stars" on its chest.

Seed-eating songsters

Finches are small perching songbirds that feed on seeds. A finch's beak is shaped like an ice-cream cone. It is short and strong and used to break open or crush the hard covering of grass seeds. Finches also catch and eat insects. When young finches hatch, they are too small to crack open seeds or eat the hard body covering of insects. Instead, both parents feed them by *regurgitation*, or spewing up food that the adult has already swallowed. This regurgitated food is soft and moist enough for baby finches to eat.

The zebra finch is Australia's smallest finch.

Reptiles
Scaly, not slimy!

Australia is home to an incredible number of these amazing vertebrates. Besides having a backbone, all reptiles are covered in scaly skin. But unlike what you may expect, their scales are dry to touch, not slimy like those of a fish. Reptiles are cold-blooded, so they need the sun to warm their bodies and give them the energy to move around.

Four groups of reptiles live in Australia — crocodiles, turtles, lizards and snakes. Many reptiles lay eggs just like birds do, but unlike birds, most reptiles don't look after their eggs or keep them warm until they hatch. Interestingly, some reptiles keep their eggs inside their body and give birth to live young.

Left: A carpet python.
Right: Australia's famous frilled lizard.

Phylum: CHORDATA
Class: Reptilia
Crocodiles 96
Freshwater turtles 98
Lizards 100
Snakes 110

Crocodiles

These reptiles could be called living dinosaurs because their body shape is almost the same as it was more than 200 million years ago! Only two types of crocodile live in Australia, the freshwater and saltwater crocodile. The freshwater crocodile is found nowhere else in the world!

Freshwater crocodile

Lizards

Most lizards have four legs — but there are always exceptions to the rule. One group of lizards, called legless lizards, have no legs at all! Legless lizards look very much like snakes, but they don't have a forked tongue!

Thorny devil

Freshwater turtles

Australia is home to turtles, but not to tortoises. You can tell the difference by looking at their feet. Freshwater turtles have webbed feet with claws, and spend most of their time swimming and hunting in the water. Tortoises have feet that look like an elephant's, and they only live on land.

Eastern snake-necked turtle

Snakes

Snakes are excellent predators, even without legs or arms! They are able to move their long, thin, muscular bodies very silently and quickly. Large belly scales help snakes to grip and push themselves along.

Diamond python

Crocodiles
Stealthy hunters

Freshwater crocodile

There are two types of crocodile living in Australia — the awesome, powerful saltwater, or estuarine, crocodile, which is sometimes also called a "saltie", and the smaller, more secretive freshwater crocodile. Both are very efficient predators that often take their prey by surprise.

Crocodiles live both on land and in the water. During the day, they bask in the sun, saving their energy for hunting at night. They are excellent swimmers, using their long tail as a paddle and their webbed feet to help pull them through the water. They can also run very quickly on land.

Above: Close-up view of a crocodile's scaly skin.

Freshwater crocodiles live only in Australia and grow to about 3 metres long. They have a narrower, more pointed snout than saltwater crocodiles.

Tough skin

A crocodile's skin is thick and bumpy. It is like an armour that helps to protect the crocodile. Crocodile skin is waterproof just like the skin of all other reptiles.

Scaly and secretive

Freshwater crocodiles only live in freshwater billabongs, swamps and rivers, where they hunt insects, fishes, frogs, lizards and birds. They have many razor-sharp teeth, but they are not considered dangerous to humans because they are quite shy and not very aggressive.

Phylum: Chordata
Class: Reptilia

Estuarine crocodiles grow up to 6 metres long and weigh over 1000 kilograms, making them the biggest reptiles on Earth!

King of the waterways

Estuarine, or saltwater, crocodiles live in saltwater estuaries and rivers, but they can also be found in freshwater billabongs, creeks, and even out in the ocean! They are ferocious, powerful predators that charge out from underwater to grab their unsuspecting prey. Dragging the animal back into the water, they roll it around underwater and drown it. Big salties take prey as large as kangaroos, wild pigs, dingoes and humans!

Sneak and stalk

Crocodiles move through the water without leaving a ripple, and only their eyes and nostrils can be seen. This enables them to stalk their prey and sneak up very close without being noticed.

Below: Crocodiles are sneaky hunters that make themselves look like a floating log.

Squeaking babies

Female crocodiles lay their eggs in a nest of mud and grass. Newborn babies have an "egg tooth" on top of their snout to help them crack open the eggshell. They squeak loudly once they hatch and their mother digs them out of the nest and sometimes carries them to the water in her mouth.

A baby crocodile.

Crocodiles launch themselves out of the water to snap at birds perched overhead.

Enormous power

The power within a crocodile's large, muscular tail can push its heavy body straight up into the air! The tail equips the crocodile with the speed to rush from the water and snatch prey. Once the chomping jaws snap together, there is rarely any escape.

Freshwater turtles
Patient paddlers

There are about 25 different types of turtle living in Australia's freshwater billabongs, wetlands and rivers. Most of a turtle's time is spent in the water hunting for food. They usually only leave their watery home to bask in the sun or to lay eggs.

When ready to lay eggs, a turtle uses its back legs to dig a hole deep enough to reach damp soil. Up to 30 eggs are dropped into the hole, which is then covered up to protect the developing young. One type of turtle, the northern long-necked turtle, lays its eggs underwater!

Eastern snake-necked turtles need to surface to breathe air.

Top: A Krefft's river turtle enjoying the sun. *Above:* The tail end of a saw-shelled turtle's shell is jagged like a saw.

Sunbaking

Turtles are cold-blooded, so when a waterhole becomes too chilly, they climb out onto a rock or log to warm themselves in the sun.

During the dry

Turtles need water to survive, so how do some freshwater turtles live in the desert? When a waterhole begins to dry up, these turtles burrow down into the damp mud. They have a special ability to curl up and sleep for a very long time without needing to eat or drink. Once the rains return and the waterhole fills up, the turtles wake up again and climb to the surface to hunt.

Phylum: Chordata
Class: Reptilia

Pig-nosed turtles live in freshwater, but have large flippers like marine turtles.

An Aboriginal rock art turtle.

Supper in a shell

The pig-nosed turtle is an important food source for the Aboriginal people of western Arnhem Land and is included in their Dreamtime stories. It is a land turtle and lives in freshwater habitats, but it has large flippers similar to a sea turtle and a bony shell covered in skin!

The western swamp turtle needs our help to survive in the wild.

A rare swamp swimmer

The western swamp turtle is the smallest of Australia's turtles. It is also the most endangered of all reptiles. Only a small number survive in the wild in swamps that have been fenced off to protect the turtles from the main threats to their survival — habitat loss, feral foxes and cats.

Squirt to divert

Although a turtle tucks its head and legs in under its shell to protect itself from predators, the snake-necked turtle also has another secret weapon. Snake-necked turtles release a smelly fluid that scares off predators!

Popular pets

The Murray River turtle can be recognised by the creamy stripe running from its mouth along the side of its head. Babies are often called "penny" turtles because of their small size, but adults can grow up to 30 centimetres long!

Murray River turtle

Lizards
Lounging sun-lovers

Lizards are probably Australia's most familiar reptiles, simply because they can often be found scampering around or sunning themselves in our own backyards. Most lizards live in dry, spinifex grasslands, but these scaly sun-seekers can live in even the hottest desert sands or the coldest snow-covered mountains!

A lizard's life depends on getting heat from the sun to warm its blood and provide it with the energy to mate, hunt and hide. During the day, lizards bask in the sunshine, but they scurry back to shade if they become too hot. Lizards that are active at night lie down on rocky surfaces which are still warm from the sun's rays and soak up the heat through their skin. Lizards belong to one of five different groups, depending on their behaviour and body features.

Phylum:	CHORDATA
Class:	Reptilia
    Legless lizards 101
    Geckoes 102
    Dragon lizards 104
    Monitor lizards 106
    Skinks 108

Left: A colourful southern forest dragon.
Above: Red-tailed dragon.

Phylum: Chordata
Class: Reptilia

Legless lizards

What has no arms or legs, looks like a snake, slithers like a snake, but is not a snake? A legless lizard! These lizards may resemble snakes but they have a fleshy, round "lizard" tongue instead of a forked tongue like a snake. Like other lizards, they also have ear openings on the sides of their heads.

Legless lizards are sometimes called "snake lizards".

Geckoes

Large, bulging eyes help these lizards search for their insect prey at night. During the day they are secretive and hide under bark, rocks or inside burrows. Geckoes lay hard-shelled, brittle eggs.

Knob-tailed gecko

Dragon lizards

Dragon lizards are good runners and climbers that rely upon their speed and their ability to blend in with their surroundings to escape from predators. Most of these lizards have a mouth full of sharp teeth with longer, dog-like canines at the front to allow them to hold on to their prey.

Eastern water dragon

Monitor lizards

Monitors are commonly called "goannas". They are different to all other lizards because these large, daytime hunters have a forked tongue, like the tongue of a snake, which constantly flickers in and out as they search for food.

Sand goannas are also called Gould's monitors.

Skinks

Skinks mainly hunt during the day. Most have smooth scales that look a little like those of a fish. When they are basking in the sun, their scales sometimes glisten with the colours of the rainbow and some have rough spiny scales along their back or tail. A few types of skink hunt at night.

This skink's scales are not all smooth.

Night stalkers

Geckoes

In north Australia, these small lizards with bulging eyes can sometimes be seen climbing along the walls and ceilings of people's houses at night. They are on the hunt, stalking insects that are attracted to the lights.

Most geckoes have thick tails that store fat. If there is no food available, the tail becomes thinner as the fat is used up to give the lizard energy. A group of geckoes known as the knob-tailed geckoes have strange, stumpy tails that end in a little ball, or "knob". When eating or resting, they use their knobby tail like a fifth leg to prop them up.

Top: Giant tree gecko. *Above right:* Wiping its eye scale. *Above left:* Some tree geckoes have curly tails that they use to grip branches as they climb.

Windscreen wipers

Geckoes don't have eyelids; they have a clear, protective scale covering their eyes — just like a windscreen! When it gets dirty, it must be wiped clean and a gecko's built in windscreen wiper just happens to be its tongue.

Sticky toes

If you had gecko toes, you could walk along your bedroom ceiling! Tiny toe ridges work like velcro to lock onto tiny ridges on the wall — even on smooth surfaces.

Centralian knob-tailed geckoes are strange looking creatures!

Desert stalker

Found in the centre of Australia, the centralian knob-tailed gecko is the largest of all geckoes and preys upon spiders, insects and scorpions. It will also stalk other geckoes! It lives and hunts on the ground, so it doesn't need sticky toes. The centralian knob-tailed gecko creeps along with slow, shaky movements until it is close enough to lunge at prey.

Phylum: Chordata
Class: Reptilia

It is hard to tell which is the head and which is the tail on this northern leaf-tailed gecko!

A leaf-tailed gecko blends in with lichen on the tree.

Camouflage

Like many other lizards, geckoes can slowly change their colour to blend in with the colours of their surroundings. Leaf-tailed geckoes use both colour and body shape to help camouflage. A leaf-tailed gecko's large tail looks like a leaf and helps it confuse predators, who can't tell which end is the head and which is the tail.

Geckoes at home

There are more than 100 different types of geckoes in Australia. They can be found along the coast, in the rainforest and in the desert. All geckoes eat insects and other small invertebrates, and some even lick the sap of trees and drink the juice of soft fruits.

Left: Knob-tailed gecko.
Below: Many geckoes survive in the harsh desert.

The hunters and the hunted

Geckoes are an important part of the food-chain because they are both predator and prey. Many other animals eat geckoes, including snakes, other lizards, nocturnal birds and mammals.

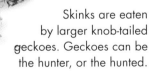

Skinks are eaten by larger knob-tailed geckoes. Geckoes can be the hunter, or the hunted.

Snakes, like the death adder (*right*) prey on geckoes.

103

The rainforest dragon is also known as the southern forest dragon.

Skilled predators

Dragon lizards

Frills, beards, spines, crests and thorns are the scaly body features that give these lizards the name "dragon". They are heat-loving hunters that search for their prey during the daytime, when insects such as grasshoppers, ants and termites are active.

Like all reptiles, dragons shed their skin. But unlike geckoes, whose skin usually comes off in one big piece, dragons shed their skin in many pieces. The skin underneath always looks fresher and more brightly coloured.

Eye spy

Dragon lizards perch in high places to watch for insects. As soon as an insect lands, the lizard leaps down and sprints to within stiking distance. If the insect stays still, the dragon can't see it, but as soon as it moves, there's a quick flick of the dragon's tongue and the insect is gobbled up.

Rainforest dragons

There are two types of rainforest dragon, but water dragons may also live in the rainforest. Rainforest dragons flatten themselves against a tree and slink around to the other side, keeping an eye on predators.

Boyd's forest dragon

The frilled lizard, Australia's largest dragon.

Big bluffers

The famous frill around the neck of a frilled lizard can be expanded like an umbrella to make the lizard look much larger and scarier than it really is. Its bright yellow mouth and loud hiss also help to bluff, or scare away, predators. If this brave display doesn't work, the lizard spins around and sprints away on its two back legs with its tail in the air.

Phylum: Chordata
Class: Reptilia

Below: The most colourful male eastern water dragons charm the most females during breeding season.

The body shape of the eastern water dragon has changed little over the past 20 million years.

Colourful displays

Eastern water dragons are often seen living by creeks and rivers in cities. During the breeding season, male dragons become much more colourful, especially around the skin on their throats. They also become much more active. They wave their arms, bob their heads and chase intruding males out of their territory.

Colour and camouflage

Dragon lizards can change the colour of their skin to suit the colour of their environment. Although the slow-moving thorny devil looks quite scary, it is not aggressive. The only way it can defend itself from predators is by its spiky skin, changing the colour of its body, and by its ability to "freeze" in position.

The colour of a thorny devil's skin changes depending on the colour of the sandy ground it lives on.

Monitor lizards

More commonly known as "goannas", the name "monitor" comes from their frequent habit of standing on their back legs with their arms hanging to the side and monitoring their surroundings. This allows them to scan for predators and prey.

Goannas are cold-blooded animals, so they only need to eat about five times their body weight in food each year. Warm-blooded animals, such as humans, certainly couldn't survive on so little food. A goanna often begins the day by poking its head out from its sleeping place to warm its brain and blood in the heat of the sun.

Clash of the titans

During the breeding season, large male monitors wrestle one another to show who's boss. The strongest wins the females and the other male's territory.

Skilled predators

Monitors are one of Australia's "top of the food chain" predators. Although they have sharp, backward-pointing teeth to grip their prey and sharp front claws to tear it to pieces, they often gulp their food whole. They eat almost anything, even dead animals, so they are almost like bush vacuum cleaners!

Lick, flick, taste

Monitors are the only lizards to have a forked tongue like a snake. Using their tongue, they pick up the scent of an animal and hunt it down by "tasting" the air and the ground.

Above and below: Yellow-spotted monitors. *Bottom right:* Frogs are one of a goanna's favourite foods.

Phylum: **Chordata**
Class: **Reptilia**

106

Mertens' water monitor

Down south

Heathland goannas and lace monitors live in cooler climates in Australia's south. To protect themselves from the cold, they stay underground in a sandy burrow or bask in the sun just outside their burrow's entrance.

A heathland goanna among pigface plants.

Freckles and lace

Lace monitors are large tree-climbers. They have powerful front legs and claws which they use to scratch a hole in termite mounds, where the female lays her eggs. When the colourful baby goannas hatch, they have a ready-to-eat meal of termites waiting for them. The freckled monitor hunts in the trees. Its body colour may change with its surroundings, but its tail is always black.

Mertens' water monitor

Like the frogs they hunt, these monitors spend much of their time in the water. They can hold their breath for a few minutes as they dive to search the bottom of a billabong or creek for yabbies, frogs and fish. In the shallows, they sweep fish closer to them using their tail.

Below left: Freckled monitor.
Left: A young lace monitor.

The Arnhem crevice skink is rarely seen.

Flashes of colour

Skinks

Skinks galore!

Skinks have conquered every habitat in Australia as a place to find food, shelter and a mate. Close to 400 different species have already been discovered!

Standing ground

The shingleback is a type of blue-tongue lizard. If it feels frightened, or if a predator is close by, it opens its wide, bright pink mouth and pokes out its thick blue tongue. It hopes to scare the intruder away by hissing and puffing its body up with air to make it seem bigger.

Small skinks are usually speedy runners and are often seen scurrying around leaves in the garden. But not all skinks are small! The blue-tongue lizard is Australia's largest skink and, at around 30 centimetres in length, is one of the biggest skinks in the world!

Some skinks lay eggs, others give birth to live young. Once the babies are born, they all brave the big wide world by themselves.

A baby rainbow skink hatching from its shell.

The shingleback lizard appears to have two heads.

A shingleback or stumpy-tail lizard.

Heads you win, tails you lose!

Shinglebacks are sometimes called two-headed lizards because their fat, stumpy tail is shaped like a head. Plus, their back feet can twist right around to face the other way, which certainly does confuse predators! The most important part of an animal's body to protect is its head. The head is also the part that a predator most wants to attack. If a shingleback can fool its enemies into attacking its tail instead, it has a much greater chance of defending itself, escaping and surviving.

Phylum: Chordata
Class: Reptilia

When breeding, male rainbow skinks become very brightly coloured.

Rainbow skinks hide under fallen leaves in the forest.

Firetail skinks twitch their bright red tails when they meet other lizards.

A flash of blue

The largest, and perhaps most easily recognised, of the skinks is the blue-tongue lizard. It has a very obvious bright-blue fleshy tongue. Blue-tongues eat both plants and animals, which makes them omnivores. They have sharp teeth and strong jaws for crunching their prey. Blue-tongues often make their homes in people's backyards, where they search for beetles and snails.

It was once believed that the blue-tongue was venomous and they can certainly give a painful bite if frightened. Research now shows that some of Australia's lizards produce a very small amount of venom in their saliva, but they don't have the fangs to inject it!

Right: A Common blue-tongue lizard.
Far right: A black whip snake feasts on a wall skink, which is being swallowed whole and headfirst!

Tasty morsels

Skinks are tasty prey for many other animals, such as birds, mammals, frogs, and other reptiles, but their excellent eyesight and lightning speed make them tricky to catch.

Snakes
Slithering strikers

Snakes are closely related to lizards, but there are some differences that set them apart. Snakes don't have arms, legs, or ears. A snake's tail is much shorter than its body, and all snakes have a forked tongue, which helps them find prey.

Snakes are carnivores and are able to swallow prey much larger than themselves, whole! Some inject venom into their prey while others squeeze their prey to death. There are six different groups of snake.

File snakes

These snakes spend their entire lives in creeks and billabongs hunting for fish. Their scales have a rough, sandpapery feel and they use their saggy skin to hold on to and squeeze their slippery prey to death.

Blind snakes

Blind snakes live underground and look like worms, but they have smooth, scaly skin and a pink, forked tongue. They have tiny eyes and can only see just enough change in the light to know whether it is daytime or night time.

An eastern brown snake.

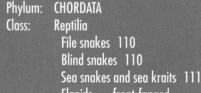

Phylum: Chordata
Class: Reptilia

Sea snakes and sea kraits

Sea snakes are close relatives of the venomous elapids that live on land, although they have paddle-shaped tails and spend most of their lives in the ocean. Their floppy bodies mean that they cannot move very well on land, so they give birth to live young in the ocean. Sea kraits are similar to sea snakes. They are also venomous and live in the ocean, but unlike sea snakes they can move very well on land and come ashore to lay their eggs.

Sea snake

Sea krait

Elapids — front-fanged snakes

Of all the snakes in Australia, this group, the elapids, is the largest. These are the venomous snakes that kill their prey by injecting it with venom, a fluid that also helps to break down the prey, or digest it, once it has been swallowed.

Tiger snake

Macleay's water snake

Colubrids — rear-fanged snakes

Colubrid snakes are found mainly in northern and eastern parts of Australia. They do not live in the central hot, dry areas or in the far south. Some resemble their deadly elapid relatives, but they have different teeth and are not considered dangerous to humans. Only four out of the ten colubrid species really have rear-fangs, the rest have solid teeth.

Pythons

The snakes known as pythons are large, powerful hunters with sharp teeth but no fangs or venom. Pythons are *constrictors*. They wrap their body around an animal and squeeze tightly. Every time the animal breathes out, the snake squeezes tighter and tighter until eventually the animal dies because it can no longer breathe in.

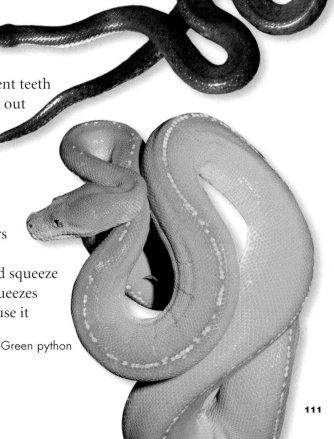

Green python

Front-fanged
Elapids

Northern death adder

Trick of the twitch!

A death adder hides under leaves with its head coiled up close to its tail. It pokes the tip of its thin tail out of the hiding place and wiggles it like a worm. Frogs, small mammals and lizards are tricked by the twitching tail and when they move closer to snatch the "worm", they get a very nasty surprise! With amazing speed the death adder's long fangs inject the animal with venom and the snake gets a very easy meal.

It may sound scary, but Australia has the highest number of venomous snakes, or elapids, in the world! In fact, there are more venomous snakes in Australia than non-venomous. Luckily, most elapids are not dangerous to humans because they are either too small to bite or live in places where they hardly ever come into contact with humans.

Many elapids are nocturnal lizard-hunters. Most lay eggs, but some, like the death adder, give birth to litters of many live young.

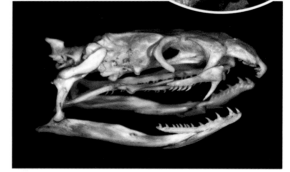

Lethal weapons

An elapid snake uses two long, hollow front teeth, called fangs, to puncture the skin like a sharp needle and either slowly drip or quickly squirt venom deep into the body of its prey. Each fang is connected to a venom gland, or sac, at the back of the snake's top jaw. This is where the venom is made. Venom kills a snake's prey in one of two ways — either paralysing the animal so that it cannot move or breathe, or destroying the animal's muscles, causing painful internal bleeding. Venom is a lethal weapon used by snakes to kill and digest prey, but it helps elapid snakes defend themselves from its predators.

Front-fanged snakes have long fangs that fold forward when the snake is ready to bite its prey.

Baby death adders leave the nest as soon as they are born.

Phylum: Chordata
Class: Reptilia

The extremely venomous taipan.

An eastern brown snake rears up, ready to defend itself from an intruder.

Ready to strike!

When it feels frightened or threatened, a snake rears up, ready to strike at its attacker. It may also flatten its neck to make it look larger than it really is.

Frog feeders

Many snakes, such as the copperhead, live around swamps, rivers and marshes where there are plenty of frogs to hunt. The spread of the poisonous cane toad has decreased the numbers of frog-eating snakes, including the red-bellied black snake.

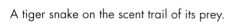

A tiger snake on the scent trail of its prey.

The "taste" of prey

Snakes use their flickering forked tongues to "taste" or "smell" the air and ground for the scent of frogs, lizards and small mammals. By following their flickering tongue, they follow the scent and catch their prey.

Copperhead

Brown tree-snakes are nocturnal.

Rear-fanged

Colubrids

Many colubrid snakes have fangs and venom, but unlike elapid snakes, their fangs are at the back of their mouths and their venom is very weak. Some colubrids don't even have fangs; instead, they have sharp, solid teeth and are not at all venomous.

Ten different types of Australian colubrids may be found living in the trees, among the mangroves or along freshwater creeks. They are sometimes called "harmless" snakes, despite often eating their prey while it is still alive!

Same snake, different colour

It can be tricky to tell which snake is which just by looking at its colour alone. The brown tree-snake above looks completely different to the one below, even though they are the same species! Some may even be shiny black in colour!

Common tree-snakes are excellent climbers.

Take to the trees

You might think it would be difficult for an animal with no arms, legs or claws to climb, but many colubrids are at home in the trees. Colubrid snakes are very muscular and their tails can also curl around twigs and branches for extra grip. The common tree-snake may even visit trees in suburban backyards as it hunt for tree-frogs.

Brown tree-snake

Phylum: Chordata
Class: Reptilia

Keelback snakes love to dine on frogs. A snake's scales stretch apart with its skin as it swallows prey often much larger than itself.

Along the creek bank

Keelback snakes live in freshwater swamps, billabongs, creeks and anywhere else they can hunt for their favourite food: frogs. Amazingly, this reptile can even eat poisonous young cane toads and still survive. Like many other colubrids that are harmless and have no venom to defend themselves, they release a very smelly fluid from their tail end to try to scare off predators.

Keelback snakes are also known as freshwater snakes.

Among mangroves and mud

There are three different snakes that make their homes among the tangled roots of mangroves where the salty sea water meets the mudflats. While the other two hide and wait for fish to swim by, the white-bellied mangrove snake slithers across the mud while the tide is out, in search of crab burrows. Once it finds a crab, it pins it down on the mud and swallows it whole.

White-bellied mangrove snake

Pythons

When hunting, pythons don't rely on speed, instead they prefer to ambush! This means they rely on camouflage and on their ability to sit and wait patiently, sometimes for days at a time, until their unwary prey comes within striking distance.

Pythons use their strength to coil around their prey and *constrict*, or squeeze, it so tightly that the animal cannot breathe and suffocates. Female pythons also use their bodies to protect their eggs, by coiling them around and "shivering" their muscles to keep the eggs warm.

No escape

Pythons don't have fangs. They have many sharp teeth that curve backwards to ensure that once they sink into prey, there is no escape. After constricting their prey, pythons swallow it whole and headfirst. A large python can even swallow a small wallaby! The water python below will slowly "walk" its top jaw, then its lower jaw over the body of the large rat it has caught until its meal has been completely swallowed.

Colour change

When they hatch, young green pythons are not actually green, but a glistening golden colour. They spend their time camouflaged high in the branches where they hunt at night for birds and mammals that feed or nest in the trees. Sometimes, they descend to low branches to ambush prey on the ground.

Phylum: Chordata
Class: Reptilia

Nature's rat traps

Carpet pythons can grow up to 4 metres in length and are probably Australia's most recognisable python. They are good climbers that will sometimes curl up inside the roofs of houses to avoid the cold. If you have a carpet python living in your ceiling, consider yourself lucky! Carpet pythons love to eat rodents and are nature's way of controlling rats.

Carpet python

Hunting heat-seekers

Most pythons hunt at night for mammals and birds. Besides a forked tongue, which detects the scent of prey, a python has deep pits along the sides of its lower lip. These pits detect heat and help the python "see" the warm-blooded, red glow of its prey in the dark. During the day, the patterns of a carpet python's scales blend in with patterns on the forest floor made by sunlight filtering through the leaves. This helps carpet pythons camouflage themselves in the daytime.

Right: Heat-sensitive pits on a python's lower jaw are called labial pits.

A steely stare

Snakes always look as if they are staring because they cannot blink! Snakes don't even have any eyelids. Instead, their eyes are protected by a clear scale. As a snake grows, it often has to shed its skin, which it peels off in one long piece, like a sock. The snake's eyescale peels off with the skin and a new one is left in its place.

Top to bottom: Scrub python; Stimson's python.

If disturbed or afraid, water pythons usually take to the water.

Rainbow snake

In sunlight, the normally dark scales of the water python glisten with rainbow colours. In Aboriginal Dreamtime stories, water pythons are the spirit of the Rainbow Serpent. Water pythons live in fresh-water billabongs and wetlands, but if these begin to dry out they move to find food. They are nocturnal hunters that feed on vertebrate animals, including baby crocodiles!

Amphibians
Life in water, life on land

Amphibians are cold-blooded, so their body temperature changes with the temperature of the outside air. They spend the first part of their life in the water as plant-eating tadpoles that breathe through gills. As adults, they live on land, are carnivores and breathe through lungs.

Frogs are the only amphibians found naturally in Australia because the cane toad is an introduced species. Australian frogs are divided into four groups, with the cane toad in a fifth group of its own.

Tadpoles (c)

A Blue Mountains tree-frog.

Phylum: CHORDATA
Class: Amphibia

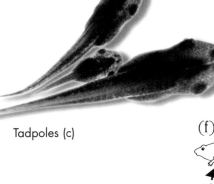

Amphibian life cycle

(a) Adult frogs mate

(b) Eggs hatch

(c) Tadpoles grow

(d) Hind legs develop

(e) Front leg emerges

(f) Other front leg emerges. The tail is absorbed, the lungs develop and the frog leaves the water.

Phylum: Chordata
Class: Amphibia

Southern frogs

The frogs that belong to this group actually live in many different parts of Australia, not just in the south. They are called "southern" frogs because they are closely related to frogs found in other countries throughout the Southern Hemisphere.

Corroboree frog

Tree-frogs and their relatives

Most tree-frogs climb and live high among tree branches in cool forests, but, amazingly, they also have some burrow-digging relatives that live deep underground in the hot, dry desert sand! Burrowing frogs, like the water-holding frog, are relatives of tree-frogs such as the orange-eyed tree-frog.

Orange-eyed tree-frog

Narrow-mouthed frogs

You could easily mistake an adult from this group for a juvenile, or young frog, because the frogs that belong to this group are tiny! The largest narrow-mouthed frog is just 4.6 centimetres long, while the smallest is a tiny 1.3 centimetres. They live in cool and damp places, often without much water. Unlike other types of frogs, they lay eggs that hatch into tiny, fully-formed frogs, rather than tadpoles.

Fry's whistle-frog

True frogs

The Australian bullfrog is the only amphibian in Australia that belongs to this group. "True" frogs are certainly not more frog-like than any other type of frog, but they were the first type of frog to be studied by scientists living in the Northern Hemisphere.

Australian bullfrog

Toads

The cane toad is the only member of the toad group living in Australia. It was brought to Australia from another country, so it is known as an "introduced species". Some frogs have bumpy skin, but the cane toad's skin is very warty and contains two large poison sacs just behind the toad's head. Cane toads also grow much larger than most frogs.

Cane toad

Bright and fancy
Southern frogs

Corroboree frog

Wearing a warning!

The spectacular colours of the corroboree frog flash a warning to predators, "don't eat me, I'm poisonous". These frogs are only about 3 centimetres long. They crawl around in tunnels underneath mountain snow and moss. Sadly, only about 300 corroboree frogs still survive in the wild.

A red-crowned toadlet.

Coastal cousin

The red-crowned toadlet is a close relative of the corroboree frog. It lives in moist forest valleys close to the coast, where it tunnels underneath fallen leaves. Like its corroboree cousin, it lays large eggs at the end of a nesting tunnel.

Phylum: Chordata
Class: Amphibia

Some of Australia's most colourful frogs belong to the group known as "southern frogs", but they are not all from the south! They live right across Australia, from burrows in the dry desert sand to snow-covered mountains, from rainforest creeks and streams to city backyards.

One place you won't find these frogs is in the trees! They all either live on the ground or under it and none of them can climb well. Unlike most other frogs, some southern frogs don't need water to breed, and will look after and protect their developing eggs and tadpoles.

Trilling frogs live underground in Australia's dry habitats. They have an amazing "sixth" sense, because they seem to know when it is going to rain! Just before the rain begins, huge numbers of trilling frogs climb out of their burrows and gather on the surface, ready to start breeding as soon as puddles appear. Their "trill" calls are high-pitched and sound like a fast rolling of your tongue against the roof of your mouth.

Below: The great barred frog is the largest of the southern frogs. *Above:* Trilling frog.

The crucifix toad is not really a toad. It is a frog with bumpy skin and a coloured cross, or crucifix, on its back.

Pobble-what? Pobblebonk!

You might think it sounds strange to call a frog a "pobblebonk", but "bonk" is the sound made when the males call out in search of females. Pobblebonks are burrowers and spend their life underground until the rains come.

Southern gastric brooding frogs may now be extinct.

Pobblebonk frogs come out to mate when it rains.

Going, going, gone?

Scientists are not sure whether this amazing species of frog, which spends its whole life in the water and incubates its eggs in its stomach, still exists. The southern gastric brooding frog hasn't been seen in the wild since 1981. The female swallows her eggs and "broods" them in her stomach, where the tadpoles develop. After about six weeks, tiny baby frogs, called "froglets", hop out of the mother's mouth.

An orange-eyed tree-frog.

Sticky fingers

Tree-frogs and their relatives

Unlike southern frogs, tree-frogs and their relatives are found throughout the world. In Australia, many tree-frogs live in wet rainforests, where they climb trees and survive on insects, but some live in a much harsher climate.

Tree-frogs have tiny ridged patterns on their toes, which help them grip smooth surfaces. They have light yet muscular bodies and loose belly skin, which helps them to cling as they climb. But not all tree-frogs climb! Some dig burrows and hide under-ground, where their skin forms a "cocoon" to stop them drying out until it rains.

Red means danger!

The bright-red colour of this tree-frog's eyes may help to protect it because the flash of red when it opens its eyes helps frighten predators away.

White-lipped tree-frogs grow very large.

Big and beautiful

At around 14 centimetres in length, this is Australia's largest frog. In fact, the white-lipped tree-frog is the largest tree-frog in the world!

The northern snapping frog, or giant frog, is *cannibalistic* — it eats its own kind!

Cannibalistic carnivores

Frogs only eat live, moving prey, including insects, small mammals, reptiles and sometimes, other frogs! Frogs have teeth, but they don't use them for chewing; instead the short spiky "teeth" on the roof of a frog's mouth are used to hold prey before it is swallowed whole, and often still alive!

Phylum: Chordata
Class: Amphibia

This Tyler's tree-frog is probably calling for a mate.

Spotlight on the climbers

Climbing tree-frogs come in all shapes, sizes and amazing colours. Some even have bumpy, warty-looking skin. They hunt at night and sleep during the day. While camouflaged in the trees, if a bug comes too close, it can be gone in a single gulp!

Below: Peron's tree-frog

Female green-eyed tree-frogs can grow almost twice as big as males.

Equipped to dig

"Tree-frogs" that prefer to burrow have hard, shovel-like edges and bumps underneath their feet to help them scoop away dirt when they spiral backwards and slowly disappear underground. About one-third of Australia's frogs burrow up to a metre below the ground where the soil is cool and moist.

The water-holding frog can store water in its body for many years.

The long-footed frog of northern Australia emerges from its burrow after rain.

A male monsoon whistling-frog guards the unhatched eggs.

On guard

A monsoon whistling-frog can grow up to 2 centimetres in length. Females lay up to 12 eggs which take around 18 days to hatch. Throughout this time, the male sits patiently, camouflaged in the soil, watching over the developing eggs.

Narrow-mouthed frogs lay eggs.

Bouncing babies

Because narrow-mouthed frogs don't need water to survive, a tadpole stage is unnecessary. Instead, they lay eggs, which hatch to reveal fully-formed baby frogs that breathe air through their lungs. During development, eggs may swell up and become three times as big as the frog that laid them!

Phylum: Chordata
Class: Amphibia

Narrow-mouthed frogs

You need good eyesight to spot these frogs because these are Australia's tiniest. Some are just over a centimetre long! They are found only in the northern parts of Australia, where the weather is warm and tropical. All of these species have narrow mouths, which gives this group of frogs their name.

These amazing frogs behave quite differently to other frogs. To begin with, narrow-mouthed frogs don't have tadpoles, their eggs hatch into tiny frogs. Females lay a small number of large, round eggs and, unlike many other frog parents, one of the parents, usually the male, stays close by until the eggs hatch.

The tapping nursery-frog is an endangered species that lives in the mountains of northern Queensland.

Tiny mouth, tiny prey

Although they are carnivores, narrow-mouthed frogs cannot fit anything too big into their tiny mouths. Ants and termites are their main food.

One of a kind

The Australian bullfrog is also known as the wood frog.

True frogs

There are more than 600 types of true frogs around the world, but Australia is home to just one, the Australian bullfrog. It grows about 10 centimetres long, but it is not the biggest "true frog". The goliath frog of Cameroon in Africa, also belongs to the true frogs group and at 30 centimetres long and weighing a whopping 3 kilograms, it is a true giant!

When a male frog croaks, it inflates the vocal sac at the front of its throat to make the noise. But when the male Australian bull-frog croaks, it inflates not one, but two vocal sacs!

A foreign invader

The cane toad

Cane toads were introduced to Australia in 1935 in the hope of controlling the sugar cane beetle pest. These large, warty, poisonous amphibians did eat some of the cane beetles, but they also ate a lot of other things! Now, their numbers have exploded and the cane toad is on a destructive path across northern and central Australia.

Australia's native frogs eat only moving prey, but the cane toad eats almost anything, including animal droppings and dog food! Cane toad adults, eggs and tadpoles are all very poisonous and many frog-eating animals die from eating a cane toad by mistake.

Top: The northern spadefoot, of the southern frog group, has bumpy skin and is often confused with a toad. *Above:* The poisonous cane toad.

Freshwater fishes
Scaly skin with slippery slime

Many of Australia's native fishes make their underwater homes inland, among reeds, tree roots and other plants in freshwater creeks, lakes and billabongs.

Like their ocean-living relatives, freshwater fishes are vertebrates and have a bony skeleton that supports their bodies and fins and helps them swim. They are cold-blooded and covered in scales like a reptile, but are slimy to touch. They don't need to come to the surface to breathe air because they have gills that filter oxygen from the water. To reproduce, fish lay eggs. Many freshwater fishes travel downstream to the salty water to breed.

Slippery eels

The long-finned eel is a slippery character. Providing there is moisture, it can slither its way over land from waterhole to waterhole! They have amazing climbing ability too, so neither rocky waterfalls or human-created weirs can stop them moving upstream. They begin and end their lives in saltwater. When a long-finned eel is old enough to breed, it travels downstream to saltwater where it lays its eggs and dies.

The slippery long-finned eel.

Phylum: Chordata
Class: Osteichthyes

Freshwater giants

Australia's largest freshwater fish is the mighty Murray River cod. The biggest ever recorded was 183 centimetres long and weighed a huge 113 kilograms! The numbers of adult Murray River cod, and all other large cod species, are now very low. To survive they need flowing, unpolluted creeks with deep pools, big boulders and "snags", or tangled roots of fallen trees, to live and breed among. They also need not to be over-fished.

A cod's mouth is huge, stretching all the way from behind the eye on one side of its head, right around to the other side. Freshwater cod are aggressive carnivores, hunting for frogs, snakes, yabbies and other fish. When the cod opens its big, wide mouth, the force of the rushing water "sucks" the prey in, and it's gone in one enormous gulp!

In clean water, a Murray River cod is a bright, speckly green colour. In muddy waters its colour becomes dull.

Yellow-finned tandan catfish live in slow-moving waterholes.

A fish with whiskers

The "whiskers" of a catfish, called *barbels*, have tiny taste-buds on them. As the catfish swims along, the whiskers taste the water and the creek bed and help the catfish search for food such as yabbies, prawns and insects.

This type of rainbowfish is only found in Utchee Creek, near Innisfail in north Queensland.

Colours of the rainbow

It is easy to see why these fish are called rainbowfish! Eastern rainbowfish live in creeks and rivers along the eastern side of Australia and their beautiful colours can change to become brighter or duller depending on the fish's size and whether it is ready to breed.

Rock bottom

Sitting motionless, like a rock on the bottom of a creek, bullrouts are very hard to see. But, you'll certainly know it if you step on one! Their top fins, side fins and underneath fins are armed with sharp, venomous spines that cause agonising pain.

Bullrouts live in slow-flowing freshwater creeks and tidal estuaries.

Spangled perch

Almighty mouth brooder

Besides helping them to gobble up other fish, crayfish and insects, the enormous mouth of the fish called "mouth almighty" has another very useful role. The male carefully carries a clutch of fertilised eggs around in his mouth for up to three weeks. Even after the baby fish hatch, they stay inside their father's mouth for a few weeks before swimming away to begin life on their own. Fish that care for their young in this way belong to a group known as "mouth brooders".

The mouth almighty fish is common in streams of north-east Queensland.

Mountain galaxias grow to 13.5 centimetres long.

Schools of perch

Native perch live together in groups, known as schools, in Australia's freshwater streams. One type, jungle perch, need shade, so they live in creeks with lots of overhanging trees. Spangled perch live almost anywhere from inland water channels to rainforest streams.

Glistening galaxias

The scales of a mountain galaxia glisten as though the fish has been covered in glitter. These beautiful fish live in the High Country, even in areas covered in snow. When hunting, they leap from the water to snap at insects that hover above the surface!

Phylum: Chordata
Class: Osteichthyes

128

Relatives of the Australian lungfish lived during the Age of Dinosaurs.

Air gulpers

Like other fishes, lungfish usually take oxygen from
the water through their gills. But, incredibly, if
their pond becomes stagnant and very little
oxygen is left in the water, they can swim to the
surface and gulp air into a sac that works like a lung to supply their
bloodstream with oxygen. Baby lungfish can even breathe through
their skin! Lungfish are omnivores. They prefer to eat frogs, fish,
worms and snails, but they also nibble on freshwater plants.

Many fishes eat insects, such
as damselflies. An archerfish
can accurately "shoot" its insect
prey from about 1.5 metres away!

Ready, aim, fire!

Archerfish are stealthy hunters. The top of an archerfish's
body is flat, so it can swim just
below the surface of the water
without causing a ripple. This
way, it can sneak up on an
insect perched on a plant above
and squirt it with high-speed
"bullets" of water droplets.
Knocked off its perch, the
insect drops into the water and
the archerfish gobbles it up!

Barramundi

Barramundi are big, powerful
fish. They can grow to lengths
of up to 1.8 metres, and live for
up to 30 years. When these fish
reach this size and age, they
are certainly female — because
barramundi start their life as
males but begin to turn into
females at about five years old.
Once they become female, they
spend the rest of their lives as
females. Barramundi live in
both freshwater and saltwater.

Barramundi can change sex!

The common archerfish is also known
as the seven-spot archerfish.

Invertebrates
Animals without backbones

The planet is crawling, fluttering, jumping, swimming and slithering with creatures that don't have a backbone. They belong to the large group of animals known as invertebrates. Unlike vertebrates, which have a backbone and a skeleton on the inside of their bodies, the skeleton of an invertebrate is on the outside and is called an *exoskeleton*!

An exoskeleton helps protect and support an animal's body, but not all invertebrates have one. Leeches and snails, for example, have soft bodies. An exoskeleton is "jointed", which means it is made up of sections that are joined together. If there were no joins, the animal would be unable to move. Invertebrates with a jointed exoskeleton are known as arthropods and make up 75 percent of all the animals on the planet! The remaining soft-bodied invertebrates can be split into two groups — worms and molluscs.

Above: Cicadas have five eyes. *Inset right:* A beautiful Ulysses butterfly.

Insects

All insects have six legs and two "feeling" antennae. The body of an insect is divided into three parts. The first, containing feeding parts, eyes and antennae, is the head. The second, the *thorax*, is where the six legs and wings join to the body. The third, the *abdomen*, is the insect's "belly".

Longicorn beetle

Arachnids — spiders and relatives

Spiders and other arthropods, such as scorpions, ticks, mites and harvestmen belong to this group. They are very different to insects. Arachnids have eight legs and only two body segments, the *cephalothorax*, which is the head and thorax joined together into one, and the abdomen.

Spiders are arachnids.

Myriapods — centipedes and millipedes

The name "myriapod" means "many feet". To belong to this group, the minimum number of feet an animal can have is 18, which means nine pairs of legs! The bodies of myriapods are made up of many segments joined together, and depending on whether it is a centipede or a millipede, each segment has either two or four legs.

Most centipedes have fewer than 100 legs.

Freshwater crustaceans

The most familiar crustaceans, such as lobsters, crabs and prawns, live in the sea, but some crustaceans also live in freshwater. These animals have a tough exoskeleton that protects their bodies. They have four antennae and their eyes sit on moveable "stalks".

Crabs have ten legs.

Worms, leeches and velvet worms

These invertebrates are not arthropods because they don't have a hard, jointed exoskeleton. Their bodies are made up of segments but the outside is soft and, for many, moist.

Leeches are bloodsuckers.

Molluscs — snails and slugs

It is hard to believe that these slimy land-living creatures are the relatives of oysters and octopuses, but all of these animals are molluscs! Most molluscs live in the water, but those that live on land have developed ways to stop their smooth bodies from drying out.

A land snail.

Ants and termites

Good things come in small packages, and these tiny insects are nature's great recyclers! Ants and termites clean up the ground by munching on fallen plants and dead animals. Their waste goes back into the soil, putting back in all of the good nutrients.

Both ants and termites may live in large city-like colonies either above or underground, but a termite is not an ant. Unlike ants, termites are blind, have straight "bead-like" antennae, are herbivorous and have a thick waist where the abdomen joins the thorax.

A bull ant.

Ant action

Ants live right across Australia, including on snow-covered mountains, sandy deserts and along rocky coasts. They have chomping jaws, called *mandibles*, and feed on plants and animals. Ants are predators and scavengers who go in search of food for their young, called *larvae*. Adult ants only eat liquid food, such as fluids from the body of their prey or sap from trees.

Blind workers

It is amazing to think that millions of tiny, blind termites (*above*) can work together to build huge, 6-metre tall, airconditioned "highrise" mounds (*left*) that stay between 25–36 degrees Celsius. Termites build rooms and corridors in their mounds to help the inside stay cool and moist, even when it is hot and dry outside.

Phylum: Arthropoda
Class: Insecta

Petite pollinators

Bees and wasps

Although some can sting, most native bees and wasps are harmless to humans and are very important to the environment because they help "pollinate" plants. Native bee honey is a valuable bush food for many Aboriginal people. Bees are herbivores, but all wasps begin life as carnivores.

A bee's head, thorax and back legs are much hairier than a wasp's. Wasps have a very thin "wasp-waist" that joins the thorax to the abdomen.

Top: Cuckoo wasps lay eggs in hunter wasps' nests. *Above:* A mud-nest building wasp on a flower.

Flower helpers

Adult bees and wasps are often seen hovering around flowers searching for nectar to sip. When they land on a flower, bees and wasps get tiny pieces of pollen stuck on their legs. They then fly off onto another flower and little bits of pollen from the flower before drop off. This process is called pollination and is how plants "reproduce" to create seeds that will one day become even more plants and flowers.

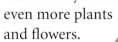

Above: Native sugar-bag bees don't sting.
Right: A blue-banded bee.

Growing up

Adult mud-dauber wasps build chambers for each of their young inside their nest of mud. The female lays an egg in each chamber and places a paralysed spider inside for the young wasp to eat as it develops and grows.

Larvae of mud-dauber wasps.

Mud-dauber wasps grow sealed inside a mud "cell".

Creepy crawlers
Beetles and bugs

Adult rhinoceros beetle.

Egg, grub, adult

When the eggs of a beetle hatch, what crawls out looks very different to the adult. A beetle spends the first part of its life as a grub, or larva, and depending on the type of beetle, is either a carnivore or a herbivore. Just like a butterfly, as the grub grows it forms a cocoon and undergoes big changes to come out shaped like an adult.

What is the difference between a bug and a beetle?
The answer is in the mouthparts. Beetles have strong "jaws" for biting and chewing their prey, while bugs have a sharp, straw-like tube which they use to pierce their food and suck its juices. Bugs also have only two wings, while beetles have four, but only two of these wings are used for flying.

The hard covers on a beetle's back are wings called *elytra*, which protect two thin flight wings underneath. When a bug hatches from its egg, it is a mini version of its parents. Beetles grow from larvae, which hatch into adult beetles.

Assassin bugs eat other insects.

Stealthy assassins

An assassin bug hides on a plant, ready to pounce on other insects. Using its piercing rostrum to stab the victim, the bug injects a paralysing fluid that turns the insect's insides into a gruesome liquid "soup" to sip!

A brightly coloured harlequin cotton bug.

Sap suckers

Many bugs use their straw-like feeding tube, called a *rostrum*, to pierce a plant's stem and suck the sweet, nutritious plant juices as food. When not feeding, they tuck their rostrum flat underneath their head. Harlequin cotton bugs eat the sap of cotton and hibiscus bushes. Females are large and orange with metallic green flecks. Males are smaller and are metallic blue with red patches.

Phylum: Arthropoda
Class: Insecta

134

Winged wizards
Mayflies, dragonflies and damselflies

Damselfly

You may encounter these dainty, daytime fliers flitting around unpolluted freshwater. They may look similar, but mayflies aren't actually related to dragonflies or damselflies at all!

Mayflies belong to the Ephemeroptera family and are the only insects that are able to fly before they become adults. Adult mayflies are small with three long tails, called *cerci*. Dragonflies use their excellent eyesight and their speed to hunt insects in flight. They can reach speeds of up to 40 kilometres an hour and can even fly backwards! Damselflies have long, straight bodies and rest with their wings above their head. Resting dragonflies hold their wings straight out from their bodies.

Nymphs

Once they hatch from their eggs, young mayflies, dragonflies and damselflies are known as nymphs. Unlike other insects, it takes most mayfly, dragonfly and damselfly nymphs a couple of years before they become adults. All nymphs spend their life in the water and breathe either through gills, through holes in their body, or through their cerci. Mayfly nymphs are herbivores that feed on algae and other plants. Dragonflies and damselflies are carnivores both as nymphs and adults. They are good insects to have around because they are great mosquito hunters.

An adult mayfly only lives for a few hours, or at most, a day!

Above: A mayfly nymph.
Right: A dragonfly nymph.

Damselflies are larger than mayflies.

Dragonflies have large eyes and very good eyesight.

Dainty delights

Butterflies and moths

A male Ulysses butterfly.

Butterfly or moth?

Moths and butterflies look alike, but there are some easy ways to tell them apart. A butterfly's antennae always end in little balls, while a moth's never do. Butterflies flutter during the day, but most moths fly at night. When sitting still, a butterfly's wings are folded together above its body, unlike a moth's wings, which lie flat.

These beautiful insects can be seen fluttering in backyards, parks, forests and in the bush. They are usually found close to a "food" plant because females lay their eggs under the leaves of the right type of food. This way, when the hungry baby caterpillars hatch from their eggs, they can begin to munch on the leaves of the food plant straight away.

If a butterfly lands on a plant and immediately flies off again, it is because the leaves of that plant are not suitable for its caterpillars to eat. Butterflies and moths "taste" the leaves with the undersides of their feet and if the taste is not right, they fly off to try the next plant.

Above: A zodiac moth.
Inset: Saturnid moth.

Rule breakers

Some moths, such as the zodiac moth, are hard to spot as moths because they look like butterflies and fly during the day.

Nectar sipping

The mouth of a butterfly or a moth is a long, straw-like tube called a *proboscis*. When they feed, the proboscis uncurls and is poked into flowers to sip the nectar. Butterflies and moths also feed on sap, damp ground, and the juices of ripe fruit. When the insect is not feeding, the proboscis curls neatly up under the insect's head.

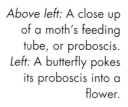

Above left: A close up of a moth's feeding tube, or proboscis.
Left: A butterfly pokes its proboscis into a flower.

Phylum: Arthropoda
Class: Insecta

The female butterfly lays an egg on the leaf of a food plant.

A hungry baby caterpillar hatches and starts to munch and munch and munch.

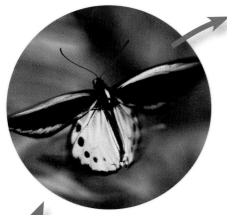

It flutters away to mate, lay its own eggs, and start the cycle of life all over again.

Life cycle of a butterfly

A butterfly's life begins as an egg laid on or underneath the leaf of a special type of food plant. When the egg hatches, the caterpillar eats the plant. As it grows, a caterpillar sheds its skin and gets bigger and bigger. When it is large enough and healthy enough, the caterpillar forms a cocoon or *chrysalis*. Inside the chrysalis, amazing changes take place and what comes out looks nothing like what went in! From egg, to spiky caterpillar, to flying adult butterfly, this is the life cycle of the Cairns birdwing butterfly.

As it grows, it becomes too big for its skin. It wriggles out of the old, small skin and keeps eating until it begins to fill out the new skin.

When all changes are complete and it breaks out of the pupa, it is no longer a caterpillar — it has transformed into a beautiful adult butterfly!

The hardened skin forms a chrysalis, or *pupa*. Tucked away inside, something incredible is happening.

When it is fully grown, it attaches itself to a leaf or twig by a silk "girdle" or thread. Hanging by the girdle, the caterpillar begins to change and its skin starts to harden.

As it sheds its skin and grows, the birdwing caterpillar changes colour.

Stick insects
are difficult to see.

Walking sticks

Phasmids and mantids

Camouflage is the key to the survival of these insects, and their various body shapes and colours certainly help. They are difficult to see when they sit very still because they blend almost perfectly with the leaves and twigs of the bushes they are sitting or climbing on.

The group known as "phasmids" is made up of stick insects and leaf insects. Phasmids are herbivores that eat leaves and plant stems. The eggs of phasmids look like woody seeds. By looking at an egg's shape you can tell exactly which type of phasmid laid the egg.

Stick insects

A long, thin body and twig-like legs help stick insects resemble part of the plant they are sitting on. Some are so thin that they look like a wispy blade of grass. Most feed at night when they can hide easily from birds and lizards.

Above: Is it a leaf, or a spiny leaf insect? *Inset:* Spiny leaf insect eggs.

Leaf insects

Spiny leaf insects are very common along Australia's eastern coast. This insect's legs are flattened like a leaf and, as it hangs from a twig, its abdomen curls up to look like a dead leaf.

There are around 160 species of praying mantid recorded in Australia so far.

Perch and pounce predators

Mantids are also called "praying mantids" (or mantises) because they perch with their front legs up, as if saying a prayer. They wait, camouflaged among the leaves for an insect to come close. As soon as one is within reach, these carnivores lunge forward, stabbing prey with their spiky front legs before devouring it piece by piece.

Phylum: Arthropoda
Class: Insecta

Bush chorus

Grasshoppers, crickets and katydids

The wonderful chirping and whirring sounds of the Australian bush are made by the males of this group of insects. Grasshoppers call to females by rubbing the spikes on their strong back legs against their wings, or grating their strong jaws together. Male crickets and katydids "sing" by rubbing their stiff front wings together.

Although some females can sing, most listen for the calls of the males. The females can hear the bush chorus very clearly through their ears, which are not on their heads, but just underneath the knee on each front leg!

Predatory katydids blend in with the colour of leaves.

Katydids

Katydids and crickets both have long antennae, live in the leaves of trees and bushes, and are nocturnal. Most feed upon leaves, seeds, fruits and pollen, but others are meat-eating carnivores.

A forest cricket.

Grasshoppers

Like crickets and katydids, grasshoppers have strong back legs which enable them to jump a long way. Some can even jump 20 times their own body length! They are always wary of predators and keep their back legs tucked up alongside their body, ready to spring to safety. To breed, grasshoppers dig a hole in the ground with the end of their abdomen and lay lots of eggs in a foamy clump.

Crickets

A female cricket pokes the long, curved tube, or *ovipositor*, at the tail end of her abdomen into the ground to lay her eggs. Many katydids also have ovipositors, and do the same.

The venomous
funnel-web spider.

Burrow-dwellers

Primitive spiders

Big and nasty

Despite being big, hairy and packed with venom, these primitive spiders are not seen very often because they are nocturnal. Males leave their burrows in search of a female only during mating season.

Primitive spiders live underground in moist tunnels that enable them to breathe through their gill-like lungs called "book lungs". Because their eyesight is not very good, they sit just at the entrance to their burrow and wait patiently for an insect to come close enough for them to see. When they do see prey, they burst from the burrow and pounce on it with amazing speed.

The burrows of these spiders are lined with silk from their abdomens, but they don't use the silk to spin a web. They sometimes nest in between cracks in rocks, logs and tree-trunks.

Funnel-web spiders rear up and pounce on prey.

Barking spiders are primitive spiders that can grow up to 6 centimetres long.

Rear and stab

Primitive spiders rear up and lunge on top of their prey, stabbing it with their long fangs to inject their venom. The power of a funnel-web's bite can help it crush its prey.

Barking spiders

Barking spiders don't actually bark! Sometimes they are called bird-eating spiders or whistling spiders, but they don't whistle and very rarely eat birds either! The name barking spider probably came about because when they are frightened they rub the two short, leg-like "palps" between their front legs along their fangs, making a sound. Barking spiders are Australian tarantulas and eat frogs, lizards and even small snakes.

Phylum: Arthropoda
Class: Arachnida

A silver-backed trapdoor spider.

Trapdoor spiders lurk near their burrows.

A funnel-web spider at its burrow entrance, ready to pounce.

Trapdoor spiders

Trapdoor spiders live in moist forests, deserts, and even in some backyards, but despite their name not all trapdoor spiders build a trapdoor. Some dig open burrows that don't have a lid, others use leaves and twigs to hide the entrance to their tunnel. Most trapdoor spiders do make a door out of soil and leaves held together by silk in a shape that fits perfectly over the burrow's entrance. This makes it nearly impossible for grasshoppers, crickets, beetles and moths to see the burrow. If they walk too close, they are dragged inside and the door is quickly slammed shut behind!

Lurking, ready to pounce

The venom of primitive spiders paralyses their prey. It shuts down the animal's nervous system and begins to turn the inside of its body into a "soup", which the spider then sucks out. Funnel-webs use their silk to set "trip-wires". They rest their front legs on the trip wire and when an animal touches the silky threads the spider gets ready to pounce.

Modern spiders

Green jumping spider with prey.

Unlike primitive spiders, the modern group of spiders have excellent eyesight, can live well away from a burrow and have invented some very interesting ways of catching their prey.

Some hunt and pounce on their prey; others set "invisible" traps that tangle, and some build beautiful strong, sticky webs. Modern spiders come in all shapes, sizes and colours. When they bite, their fangs work like a pair of tweezers to grip and move their prey around. The squeezing force can be so strong that it can sometimes even crush an insect's body!

Spring-loaded

One of the most colourful groups of spiders, the jumping spiders, are daytime stalkers. They see their prey, creep to within pouncing distance, and then leap using the power of their back legs to seize their catch.

A female red-back spider has a red splash on her back.

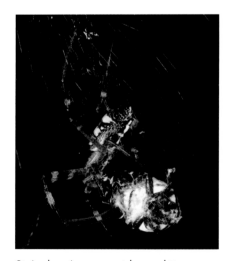

St Andrew's cross spider and its prey.

Red marks the spot

The red-back is probably Australia's most easily recognised spider because of the bright splash of red on its hairy black or brown abdomen. Red-backs often live around houses and buildings, but they are shy and not often seen. They build a low web and stretch lines of silk down to the ground. If a small beetle or insect touches one of these lines, just like a rubber band the silky line flings back up into the web, taking the beetle with it.

Sticky silk

Some spiders make webs of sticky silk to catch their prey. Once stuck in the web, there is little chance of prey escaping.

Phylum: Arthropoda
Class: Arachnida

A wolf spider carries its spiderlings on its back.

Huntsman spiders can give a painful bite.

The wolf and the huntsman

The wolf spider and the huntsman are large, predatory arachnids that hunt down their prey. Wolf spiders live on the ground and hide beneath fallen leaves or inside burrows. Huntsman spiders use their flattened bodies to sneak in between cracks in rocks and under bark on tree trunks. Unlike most spiders, whose legs bend upwards as they walk, the huntsman's legs bend forward and it scurries along the ground like a crab. Unusually for spiders, a mother wolf spider takes care of her baby "spiderlings", carrying them around on her back until they are old enough to look after themselves.

Water spiders sit on the water's surface, waiting to plunge down and grab prey from below.

Eye spy

Spiders usually have six or eight eyes. Wolf, huntsmen and jumping spiders are hunters with eyes placed so that they can be on the look-out for prey, and predators, in every direction.

No web needed

Amazingly, water spiders can run across the surface of streams and ponds without sinking! As they sit on top of the water, their feet can feel vibrations. If a tadpole or small fish swims below, the spider quickly dives below to catch its prey. If an insect drops into the water, the spider sprints across the surface and grabs it.

Bird-dropping spiders are brown, white and shiny. They get their name because they look just like a wet bird poo. This is great camouflage from predators, but they also use it to attract prey, because they even smell like poo! Poo-eating insects like flies, are drawn to the smell and soon find out that this particular "bird dropping" has fangs!

Above left: A wolf spider.
Above: A bird-dropping spider.

Stingers and burrowers

Spider relatives

Some common relatives of spiders also belong to the arachnid group. These are the scorpions, ticks, mites, harvestmen and creatures that look like scorpions called "pseudoscorpions", which means "fake scorpions".

Just like spiders, these arachnids also have eight legs and only two body parts, although the body of a harvestman almost looks like one complete oval. Spider relatives have jaws that work like pinching clamps and are able to puncture their prey and suck its bodily fluids.

Above and inset right: Scorpions have a stinging tail.

Scorpions

Scorpions hunt centipedes and insects. They use their nipping claws, or *pincers*, to hold their prey and crush it. While the pincers grip the prey tightly, the scorpion bends its tail overhead to sting the prey and inject it with venom.

Pseudoscorpions don't have a stinger.

Scorpion look-alikes

Pseudoscorpions hunt for mites. They have paralysing venom in their pincers instead of a stinging tail like "true" scorpions.

Glowing exoskeleton

Scientists who study scorpions and their behaviour have an easy way of tracking down these night-time hunters — they use ultraviolet light! Under ultraviolet light, the tough outside skeleton of a scorpion glows an eerie blue-green. Why a scorpion "glows" under ultraviolet light is still unknown, but it may be a way for the scorpion to detect, and stay away from, harmful levels of daytime sunlight, or ultraviolet rays.

Phylum: Arthropoda
Class: Arachnida

Velvet mites get their name because their many tiny hairs make them look "velvety".

Mites

Mites are tiny, round-bodied animals. Some are carnivores that hunt other mites, others eat plants, fungi, farm crops, leaves and the juices of fruits. There are even some types of mite that live under the skin of humans, or in our homes and beds where they feed on tiny flakes of skin that fall off our bodies every day! Other mites also play an important environmental role by eating dead animals and putting their nutrients back into the soil.

Harvestmen

With a body of only about a centimetre in length and eight very long, thin legs, harvestmen are often mistaken for daddy long-legs spiders. But they are definitely not spiders! Harvestmen live in moist forests where they hunt among the fallen leaves for insects and other small invertebrates. Their fangs are small and look more like claws.

Ticks

Ticks are *parasites*. They attach themselves to a "host" animal to feed on blood. They climb up a blade of grass and wait for a victim, like a kangaroo or a human, to come close enough for them to "jump aboard". Their piercing straw-like mouth punctures their victim's skin and its special backwards-facing hooks make sure that the tick stays attached. As ticks drink their fill, their abdomen swells with blood, like a huge, gruesome balloon.

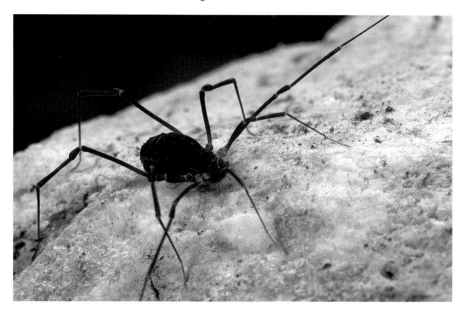

Harvestman are gangly, long-legged spider relatives.

Scrub ticks can make humans feel quite sick.

Lots and lots of legs

Centi-speeds

Packed with pace, house centipedes run at speeds of 50 centimetres a second. They have 30 legs, but only eight ever touch the ground at the same time. They are called house centipedes because they are mainly seen scurrying around houses after spiders and insects.

Centipedes and millipedes

The word "centipede" means "100 feet", but the centipedes living in Australia have fewer than 100 legs, while some species in other countries have many more. "Millipede" means "1000 feet", and while no millipede actually has 1000 feet, most millipedes in Australia have more than 60 legs and some overseas have more than 700!

Millipedes and centipedes have tough exoskeletons that protect their bodies. This outside skeleton is divided into many sections. Centipedes have one pair of legs branching out from each body section, or segment, but millipedes have two pairs.

Left: A house centipede is sometimes also called a "Johnny hairy legs".

Above: Millipedes can grow up to 12 centimetres long.

Don't run, dig!

You might think that because millipedes have lots of legs, they must be fast runners — not so! But they are fast burrowers and can disappear headfirst under the forest floor.

Smelly defence

Millipedes are scavenging herbivores that feed on rotting plants, fungi and wood. They don't have venomous fangs, so instead they defend themselves from attack by squirting a smelly, coloured liquid that is hard to rub off.

Phylum: Arthropoda
Class: Chilopoda (Centipedes)
Class: Diplopoda (Millipedes)

Scolopendrid centipedes have 21 pairs of legs.

Venomous fangs

Centipedes are ferocious carnivores that hunt other animals such as insects, spiders, and even scorpions. They have very strong jaws, or fangs, that inject venom to paralyse their prey. Their two long, colourful back legs don't sting but are used to grip prey.

A close-up of a centipede's puncturing fangs.

Below left: Scolopendrid centipede eggs. *Below right:* Newly hatched scolopendrid centipedes.

Egg laying

Centipedes lay their eggs under rocks or logs. Many mothers even coil their bodies around the eggs to protect them from predators. After hatching, some young look like miniature versions of their parents, others may need to grow more legs and length.

Clawed creek-dwellers

Freshwater crabs, crays, yabbies and prawns

A freshwater crab.

Waiting for rain

Some freshwater crabs live in creeks and dams far inland, where it is hot and dry. If there is a drought during the spring breeding season, a female carries her eggs on her belly and stays in her moist, deep burrow until the rains come and there is enough water for the young to hatch and begin the search for food.

Crabs, crays, yabbies and prawns are invertebrates that have ten legs, including their two large front legs, which are equipped with strong claws for nipping and picking up food. They have four antennae, two long and two short, which are used as "feelers". Their moveable eyes sit on stalks above their heads and they breathe through gills like fish.

A hard shell, or exoskeleton, supports and protects their soft bodies. As they grow, they *moult*, or shed their exoskeleton like a snake sheds its skin. The new shell underneath is very soft and until it hardens they must stay hidden from predators.

The "destructor" yabby, or blue claw, can ruin dam walls with its digging.

Lamington spiny crayfish live only in high-altitude streams in south-east Queensland.

Survival strategies

Yabbies are a type of crayfish. To stay alive during a drought, they burrow into a moist, muddy bank to keep cool until the rains arrive. The burrows of "destructor" yabbies cause lots of damage to the walls of farm dams.

Mountain blues

The bright-blue and white lamington spiny crayfish lives in cool mountain streams on the Lamington Plateau. They sit on the rocky creek bottom, munching on fallen leaves and decaying plants.

Phylum: Arthropoda
Class: Malacostraca

148

Egg protection

A female crayfish can lay hundreds of eggs. While the eggs are developing, she carries them around with her under her folded-up tail! In warm summer months, crayfish sometimes venture out of the water and wander across the damp forest floor. If they feel frightened, they put on a scary display by waving their pincers, loudly clacking and snapping their claws and hissing loudly to try and frighten away predators.

Above: A female Mount Lewis crayfish giving a claw-clacking defensive display. *Left:* Small, ball-like crayfish eggs are kept under the tail.

Freshwater prawns scavenge on the river bed for food.

Free swimmers

Unlike crayfish and crabs, which move around by walking and crawling, prawns like to swim. Once a female lays her eggs, she doesn't protect them under her tail. Instead, they drift off into the water and must survive on their own.

The Sydney crayfish is a spiny cray.

Spiky armour

Some freshwater crays have large spikes on their claws and tail. They belong to a group known as spiny crayfish, which live in fast-flowing streams where the bubbling water has a lot of oxygen.

Swallow, suck and rip
Worms, leeches and velvet worms

A close-up of a velvet worm.

Moist habitats are home to these soft-bodied invertebrates that live in soil or on the forest floor among the leaves and decaying wood. Worms and leeches are grouped together because of their round, cylinder-shaped bodies. Velvet worms, although called "worms", are very different.

Despite their soft, gentle look, velvet worms are savage hunters. When they catch their invertebrate prey, they immobilise it with a sticky mucus and then rip it open and drink its insides! Earthworms are burrowers that swallow soil as they move along underground, while leeches suck blood from their prey.

A worm with legs!

Velvet worms look and behave more like centipedes than worms. They have two antennae, chomping jaws and many legs to crawl across the forest floor at night in search of prey.

A garden earthworm (*top*) and a rainforest earthworm (*right*).

Blood-suckers

If you go bushwalking in places where it is damp and moist, watch out for these little suckers. Leeches are always on the lookout for a feed of blood. One good meal can fill a leech's body enough that it doesn't need to eat again for months!

Busy burrowers

Earthworms are fabulous gardeners! They gulp down soil and rotting plants while they tunnel underground. Earthworm tunnels help oxygen and water seep into the soil to reach the roots of mosses and plants. Worm poo is called *wormcasts* and acts like a natural fertiliser for the surface of the soil.

A leech waits, ready to latch on to a passer-by.

Phylum: Annelida
Class: Oligochaeta (Earthworms)
Class: Hirudinea (Leeches)

Phylum: Onychophora
Class: Onychophora (Velvet worms)

150

Smooth and slimy
Snails and slugs

You can tell where a snail or slug has slithered by following its shiny, zig-zag trail of "slime", or mucus. The mucus keeps the body moist and provides a slippery surface that makes gliding along the ground smooth and easy.

Slugs look like snails without a shell and prefer moist habitats to stop their soft skin from drying out. Snails also like moisture, but because they have a shell for protection, some can even live in the desert. Most snails and slugs are omnivores that use their tongue, or *radula*, which is covered in many tiny teeth, to eat plants and dead animals.

Semi-slugs blend in with the forest floor.

Tiny shell

Although difficult to see, semi-slugs have a small shell, which their bodies are too big to fit into. To protect themselves, these slugs rely on tricking their predators. They "drop" their tail, which begins to wriggle like a worm. While the predator attacks the tail, the slug slides away.

Snails leave a slippery trail of mucus as they travel along.

A spiral home

As a snail grows, a hard shell coils around its body to form a "home" to protect it from predators. If a snail's habitat begins to dry out, it can tuck its body away inside its shell and plug the entrance with slimy mucus. This plug helps keep the snail's body moist but still allows oxygen in so that the snail can breathe.

Land snail

Up periscope!

The eyes of slugs and snails are on the ends of long stalks called tentacles. They can pull their eyes in close to their heads to protect them or extend them like a periscope to look in all directions.

Phylum: Mollusca
Class: Gastropoda

Changing the balance

Settling of humans, unsettling of wildlife

If you lived in Australia around 220 years ago, you would have been living with many more animals than you are able to see today. Since the arrival of the early European settlers, some animals have become extinct and others have become much rarer. The balance of Australia's native wildlife has changed in a big way and, unfortunately, for many species, this change is forever.

Early settlers didn't always realise that clearing habitats to create farms was also destroying animals' homes. Also, bringing animals from other countries into Australia meant native animals suddenly had to compete with fast-breeding, skilful hunters they had never seen before.

Before early settlers arrived, there were many bridled nailtail wallabies, eastern quolls (*right*) and numbats in Australia; now these are endangered species.

What can we do to help native wildlife?

Wildlife carer: By volunteering as a wildlife carer, you could help look after a sick, injured or orphaned animal and get closer than ever to some furry, scaly or feathery friends. To find out more go to **www.wildcare.org.au/html/carers07.htm**

Nest boxes: Your home can also be a home for animals like parrots, possums, bats and owls if you create warm, safe nest boxes where they might sleep. Visit the following site and type in nest boxes wildlife for instructions. **www.dpi.vic.gov.au/dpi/index.htm**

Pet patrol: By keeping cats and dogs inside at night, you will help keep native wildlife around your home safer, and your pet will be safer too! Visit **www.wires.org.au/education_pet.htm** to find out more.

Native flowers: One way to have a backyard that is busy with bees, birds, butterflies and other wildlife is to plant native plants. The flowers of native trees and bushes attract many daytime animals, as well as some nocturnal feeders such as possums and bats. Because native plants are used to the harsh Australian environment, a bush garden also needs very little water. A visit to your local native plant nursery will help you decide which plants will make your garden wildlife friendly.

Frog friendly: If you like hearing the croaks, chirps, bonks and tinks of frogs in your garden at night, build them a pond in your backyard or simply make your backyard a frog-friendly zone and avoid using fertilizer and pesticides. **www.frogs.org.au/frogwatch/friendly.html**

Feral animals

Brought into Australia from other countries as pets or as farm animals, these "domesticated" animals escaped, went bush and turned feral. They now live and hunt in the bush and affect the balance of Australia's native wildlife in many ways. To find out more visit **www.feral.org.au**

Cats

Feral cats breed very quickly.

Over 100 years ago, cats were deliberately set loose in the bush in an attempt to decrease the numbers of rats, mice and rabbits. Unfortunately, these nocturnal predators also have a taste for native mammals, birds and reptiles, and because they can give birth to as many as fifteen kittens a year, their numbers have exploded.

Rabbits

Rabbits were first released for hunting.

First released for "sport", as an animal for settlers to hunt, rabbits are now one of the most widespread and destructive mammals in Australia.

Foxes

The European red fox eats many small mammals.

Sneaky foxes prey upon many native animals and have especially caused a huge decrease in the numbers of native mammals. They even dig up and eat the eggs of nesting sea turtles!

Goats

Feral goats cause over-grazing and soil erosion.

Almost 3 million feral goats live among dry rocky hillsides across much of Australia. They push native animals out of their living spaces and eat native plants, destroying natural habitats.

Cane toads

Cane toads poison many frog-eating native animals.

These poisonous large amphibians kill any native wildlife that mistakes them for frogs, they also prey upon any animals small enough to fit in their mouths.

Pigs and buffalo

Feral pigs destroy native vegetation.

Both of these animals muddy up rivers and wetlands and increase the spread of disease in native wildlife populations.

Close encounters

Coming face-to-face with wildlife

Getting out and about in the natural environment can provide many memorable wildlife experiences. The easiest, and sometimes closest, encounters may come by simply visiting a zoo, sanctuary or wildlife park where you can safely come face-to-face with some of Australia's most adorable creatures. You may also have the chance to touch some animals, such as reptiles, that you never dreamt you could, or would!

Being close to native animals helps you develop a greater understanding of the way they behave, what they like to eat, and how they defend themselves from predators. A close encounter with Australia's wonderful wildlife is an amazing experience, and one thing is certain — you can never be too young or too old to enjoy it!

Getting close to a furry native animal is an exciting experience at any age.

At a wildlife park, you might be lucky enough to hold a scaly skink like the blue-tongue lizard above.

Many animals in zoos or sanctuaries are used to humans.

This common wombat enjoys visits from humans.

You may even get the chance to see a tawny frogmouth!

Getting close to animals is a great way to learn about them.

Encountering the endangered

Some native animals are endangered in the wild. Zoos and sanctuaries play a very important role in breeding these animals to stop them from becoming extinct. Many animals are kept in enclosures, or areas, designed to be just like their natural habitats, allowing them to breed, eat and behave just like they would in the wild. This also provides a fabulous opportunity for humans to watch and learn all about animals they may never see in the wild.

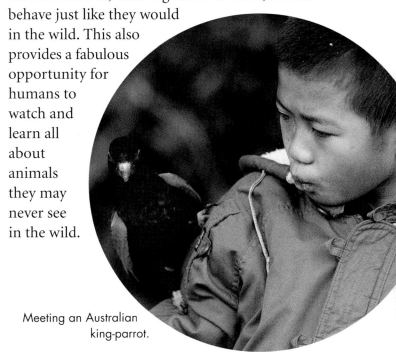
Meeting an Australian king-parrot.

Junior wildlife rangers

If you like adventure and enjoy exploring the environment, perhaps you should think of becoming a junior wildlife ranger! Many zoos, sanctuaries, wildlife parks and national parks run junior ranger programs where you can learn how to look after native wildlife and protect the environment. Every program is different, but you might get to help prepare an animal's food, spend time with veterinarians, or go behind the scenes to get closer to native animals than most people ever will. You might go bushwalking, spotlighting, or even animal trapping. And who knows, maybe one day you'll become a senior ranger and have close encounters with native animals every day!

Glossary

amphibian A four-limbed, cold-blooded animal that lives both on land and in water over its life cycle.

ancestor A relative from many hundreds of thousands of years ago

antenna (plural: **antennae**) Slender, sensitive feelers.

anus The final opening of the digestive canal of an animal.

asexual reproduction When a new individual is formed from a single parent organism without any sexual process.

bacteria Tiny single-celled organisms.

basking Lying in a sunny place.

barbels Slender, fleshy feelers around the mouths of some types of fish.

book-lungs A pair of breathing structures of arachnids made up of two cavities containing double-walled leaves between which blood circulates.

breed To have young ones that can also have their own children.

broods Sits on eggs.

camouflage Colouring that helps an animal blend in to its backgound.

cannibal An animal that eats others of its own species.

carapace A hard shell that covers the top and sides of an animal's body

carnivore An animal that eats meat and other animals.

carrion Dead, rotting flesh.

cartilage Flexible connective tissue.

cephalothorax The combined head and thorax of some crustaceans and spiders.

chrysalis Hard-shelled pupa of a butterfly or moth.

cilia Fine, hair-like structures.

crepuscular An animal that is active at dusk or dawn.

crustacean A shellfish, such as a crab or prawn.

colony A group of the same kind of animals living together.

digit A finger or toe.

diurnal Active during daylight hours.

ectothermic "Cold-blooded". An animal whose body heat remains close to the temperature of its environment.

elapid A snake with hollow front teeth that are used to inject venom.

elytra A pair of hard, front wings of some insects that forms a covering for the softer back wings.

endothermic "Warm-blooded". An animal that can maintain its own body heat.

exoskeleton The protective covering on the outside of the body of some invertebrates.

extinct Having no living examples of the same kind, or species.

feral Having gone wild.

gills Breathing organs for animals that live in water.

habitat Where an animal lives.

herbivore An animal that eats plants.

incubate To keep eggs at the right temperature for hatching young.

insectivore An animal that eats mainly insects.

introduced species Brought into one country from another country where it originated.

invertebrate An animal that does not have a backbone.

larva (plural: **larvae**) The grub or caterpillar that hatches from a butterfly or moth egg.

macropods A group of herbivorous Australian marsupials with big, strong hindlegs.

marsupium A pouch of skin on the belly enclosing the nipples.

mandible Jaws (or the mouthparts of crustaceans and insects).

mate When a male animal transfers special cells to a female's eggs, which causes young ones to develop.

megafauna Very large animals that were present in Australia until perhaps 20,000 years ago.

membrane Sheet-like connective tissue.

mollusc An invertebrate animal with a soft body and, usually, a shell.

moult To shed hair, feathers, skin or shell.

mucus A slimy substance produced by some animals.

nectivore An animal that eats nectar.

nocturnal Active at night.

omnivore An animal that eats plants and other animals.

ovipositor A pointed organ that some female animals use to deposit eggs.

parasite An animal or plant that lives on or in another species (the host) and takes nourishment from them.

patagium A thin membrane stretching down both sides of the body which allows an animal to glide through the air.

placenta A structure that connects the circulatory system of an unborn baby to its mother.

pollination A way in which plants reproduce.

predator An animal that hunts and eats other animals.

preen When a bird uses its beak to keep its feathers clean and tidy.

prehensile Capable of grasping.

proboscis A long, tubular snout or feeding organ.

pupa (plural: **pupae**) An inactive, immature stage between larva and adult.

radula Rasp-like tongue of most molluscs.

scavenger To eat carrion.

spawn Eggs and sperm of frogs, fishes and aquatic invertebrates.

spicule A small, slender, sharp-pointed body part.

syrinx The vocal organ of birds.

thorax The chest region of vertebrates and the region between the head and abdomen of invertebrates.

toxic Poisonous.

venom Poison made by animals that can be injected into prey.

vertebrae More than one of the bones in a backbone or spine.

vertebrate An animal that has a backbone.

zygodactylous Having two pairs of toes, one pair at the front of the foot and one pair at the back.

Index

Photo Credits

Front cover: Harlequin Cotton Bug and Ulysses Butterfly both by Michael Cermak.

Inside front cover: Ulysses Butterflies Michael Cermak.

p. 2: Gary Bell/OceanwideImages.com

p. 6: pterosaur © Queensland Museum, artist Paul Lennon; *Minmi* photograph © Queensland Museum/Bruce Cowell; *Genyornis* and *Procoptodon* © Queensland Museum, artist Paul Lennon

p. 7: Age of Dinosaurs mural © Queensland Museum, artist Sally Elmer; Dromaeosaurs © Queensland Museum, artist Paul Lennon; fossil dig photo © Queensland Museum/Gary Cranitch

p. 10: dragonfly, Stanley Breeden

p. 13: coral grunter, Michael Cermak

p. 19: platypuses (top and bottom left) Gary Bell/OceanwideImages.com; platypus egg, Dr Tom Grant

p. 22: allied rock-wallaby, Martin Willis; marsupial mole, Bruce Thomson/ANTphoto.com

p. 24: common planigale, mulgura, both by Ian Morris.

p. 25: phascogales in pouch, brush-tailed phascogale, Ian Morris

p. 26: western quoll, Jiri Lochman/Lochman Transparencies

p. 27: spotted-tail quoll Gary Bell/OceanwideImages.com

p. 31: baby numbats (centre left) Jiri Lochman/Lochman Transparencies; baby numbats (top right), Michael Morcombe;

p. 32: northern brown bandicoot, Ian Morris

p. 36: koala (centre left) Gary Bell/OceanwideImages.com

p. 37: koala and joey (top left) Gary Bell/OceanwideImages.com

p. 40: feathertail glider, Martin Willis; honey possum, Michael Morcombe

p. 41 squirrel glider (top right) Hans & Judy Beste/Lochman Transparencies

p. 42: common brushtail possum (top), Gary Bell/OceanwideImages.com

p. 45: allied rock-wallaby, Martin Willis

p. 47: baby joey (centre right) Jiri Lochman/Lochman Transparencies

p. 49: Cape York melomys, Michael Cermak

p. 50: diadem leafnosed bat (top left), Ian Morris

p. 51: flying fox colony, spectacled flying fox both by Michael Cermak

p. 52: Queensland pebble-mound mice, Michael Cermak

p. 53: prehensile-tailed rat, Michael Cermak

p. 54 dingo pack (centre left) Gary Steer

p. 55: all images by Gary Steer

p. 61: cassowaries (top) Martin Willis

p. 65: black-necked stork chicks (bottom right) and stork with chick (top right) both taken at Rainforest Habitat, Port Douglas.

p. 69: all images by Martin Willis

p. 73: all images by Martin Willis

p. 75: comb-crested jacana, Belinda Wright

p. 76: red-necked avocet, Peter Slater; beach stone-curlew and red-capped plover both by Martin Willis

p. 81: southern boobook owl, Hans & Judy Beste

p. 82: forest kingfisher, Peter Slater; dollarbird, Martin Willis

p. 83: all blue-winged kookaburra images by Martin Willis

p. 84: variegated fairy-wren, Peter Slater

p. 86: noisy pitta, Martin Willis

p. 87: all images by Len H. Smith.

p. 88: nestling (top left), crimson chat (top right), Martin Willis

p. 89: golden whistler, yellow-bellied sunbird, rufous fantail all by Martin Willis

p. 90: tooth-billed bowerbird, golden bowerbird, both by Martin Willis; male satin bowerbird (top right) Ken Stepnell

p. 91: great bowerbirds (bottom left and right), Martin Willis

p. 93: double-barred finch, Martin Willis; zebra finch, Peter Slater.

p. 99: western swamp turtle, Jiri Lochman/Lochman Transparencies; Aboriginal rock art turtle photograph, Ian Morris

p. 100: red-tailed dragon, Ian Morris

p. 102: centralian knob-tailed gecko, gecko toes, both by Ian Morris

p. 103: death adder, Ian Morris

p. 104: Boyd's forest dragon, Michael Cermak

p. 106: yellow-spotted monitors (bottom left) and monitor with frog (bottom right) both by Ian Morris

p. 107: freckled monitor, Ian Morris

p. 108: baby rainbow skink, Ian Morris

p. 109: rainbow skinks (top left and right), firetail skink, black whip snake, all by Ian Morris

p. 110: eastern brown snake, Michael Cermak; file snake and blind snake both by Ian Morris

p. 111: sea krait, Ian Morris; Macleay's water snake, Michael Cermak

p. 112: baby death adders, Ian Morris; snake eating gecko, and snake fangs, both by Michael Cermak

p. 113: eastern brown snake, Michael Cermak

p. 114: brown tree-snake (top left), Stanley Breeden; brown tree-snake (bottom left) and common tree-snake both by Ian Morris

p. 115: keelback snake (top), Michael Cermak; keelback snake (centre right) and white-bellied mangrove snake both by Ian Morris

p. 116: young green python (inset); snake jaw, snake eating rat both by Ian Morris

p. 117: python's labial pits (centre right) Ian Morris

p. 118: all images by Ian Morris

p. 119: southern corroboree frog, Fry's whistle frog, Australian bullfrog all by Ian Morris

p. 120: corroboree frog, red-crowned toadlet, great barred frog all by Ian Morris

p. 121: crucifix toad, pobblebonk frog both by Ian Morris

p. 122: northern snapping frog, Ian Morris

p. 123: female green-eyed tree-frog, water-holding frog and long-footed frog, all by Ian Morris

p. 124: monsoon whistling frog, narrow-mouthed frog egg both by Ian Morris; tapping nursery frog, Michael Cermak

p. 125: Australian bullfrog and northern spadefoot both by Ian Morris

p. 126: long-finned eel (left), Michael Cermak; eel (bottom right) Gary Bell/OceanwideImages.com

p. 127: yellow-finned catfish, rainbowfish both by Michael Cermak

p. 128: bullrouts, mouth almighty, spangled perch all by Michael Cermak; mountain galaxias (centre right and inset) both by Gary Bell/OceanwideImages.com

p. 129: damselfly, barramundi, common archerfish all by Michael Cermak

p. 130: all images by Michael Cermak

pp. 131–134: all images by Michael Cermak

p. 135: damselfly, Stanley Breeden; all others by Michael Cermak

p. 136: zodiac moth, Peter Slater; male Ulysses butterfly, saturnid moth and close-up of proboscis all by Michael Cermak

p. 137–139: all images by Michael Cermak

p. 140: funnel-web spider (top left) Jiri Lochman/Lochman Transparencies; funnel-web spider (bottom left) and barking spider (centre right) both by Michael Cermak

p. 141–150: all images by Michael Cermak

p. 151: snail etch (top left) Ian Morris; all others by Michael Cermak

About the Author...

Kylie Currey grew up on a dairy farm in the Gold Coast hinterland, which inspired her appreciation of wildlife and her love of exploring the environment. She has two university degrees, in science and education, and taught biology in high schools before working as an education officer in a Gold Coast wildlife sanctuary. Following that, she worked as a presenter on a children's ecology-based television program before writing and creating product for Steve Parish Publishing.

About Steve Parish...

Steve Parish has always enjoyed exploring the natural world around him and it was his enthusiasm for diving that inspired him to take his first photograph, underwater, when he was 16 years old. From that moment on, photography and the challenge of capturing the unique life forms, landscapes and colours of Australia became Steve's passion. Forty years on, Steve still travels Australia photographing. These days he also likes to spend his creative energies writing, inspiring and educating people worldwide through his photographic books about the natural wonders of Australia.

Acknowledgments

Firstly, I would like to extend my gratitude to Michael Cermak (MSc Zoology and Ecology) for providing a comprehensive review of the final manuscript and for granting access to many of his own outstanding wildlife photographs.

Secondly, I would like to thank the many zoologists, naturalists and animal keepers who have generously assisted me in accessing some very shy and timid creatures over a great many years of wildlife photography.

Thanks to the Queensland Museum for allowing us to use some of their excellent, accurate illustrations of prehistoric life and photographs of fossils.

Thanks also to the staff of the Rainforest Sanctuary at Port Douglas for allowing me to photograph their nesting Black-necked storks and chicks — the first to be bred in captivity in Australia.

My special thanks must go to my own staff, who have worked particularly hard to bring this book to fruition.

Published by Steve Parish Publishing Pty Ltd
PO Box 1058, Archerfield, Qld 4108 Australia
www.steveparish.com.au
© Steve Parish Publishing Pty Ltd

ISBN 978174021799 6
First published 2006. Reprinted 2007, 2008.

Photography: Steve Parish
Additional photography as credited on p. 159
Text: Kylie Currey
Design: Gill Stack, SPP
Editing: Britt Winter; Karin Cox, SPP
Production: Tiffany Johnson; Tina Brewster, Jacqueline Schneider, SPP
Prepress by Colour Chiefs Digital Imaging Pty Ltd, Brisbane, Australia
Printed in Singapore by Craft Print International Ltd
Produced in Australia at the Steve Parish Publishing Studios